Empire Builders

VALERIE SIMONEAU

EMPIRE BUILDERS

SYSTEMS and MODELS for BUILDING a SUCCESSFUL REAL ESTATE BUSINESS

NEW YORK

LONDON • NASHVILLE • MELBOURNE • VANCOUVER

Empire Builders

Systems and Models for Building a Successful Real Estate Business

© 2022 Valerie Simoneau

Published in New York, New York, by Morgan James Publishing. Morgan James is a trademark of Morgan James, LLC. www.MorganJamesPublishing.com

Proudly distributed by Ingram Publisher Services.

Morgan James BOGO™

A **FREE** ebook edition is available for you or a friend with the purchase of this print book.

_____

CLEARLY SIGN YOUR NAME ABOVE

Instructions to claim your free ebook edition:
1. Visit MorganJamesBOGO.com
2. Sign your name CLEARLY in the space above
3. Complete the form and submit a photo of this entire page
4. You or your friend can download the ebook to your preferred device

ISBN 9781631955921 paperback
ISBN 9781631955938 ebook
Library of Congress Control Number:
2021935618

Cover Design by:
Christopher Kirk
www.GFSstudio.com

Morgan James is a proud partner of Habitat for Humanity Peninsula and Greater Williamsburg. Partners in building since 2006.

Get involved today! Visit MorganJamesPublishing.com/giving-back

This book is dedicated to my husband, Jason.

CONTENTS

INTRODUCTION

A s I sit here and reflect back on the last five years of my career, I wonder what my life would have been like if I didn't take this career path. I wonder if I would be the confident woman I stare at in the mirror every morning.

I refuse to allow anyone in an Administration role in Real Estate to think they are just in a job. We have an opportunity to build a career, and when partnered with the right people and team leader it will flourish into an amazing career.

I wrote Empire Builders in hopes to bridge the gap between Admin and Agent. To

help both build systems together. I have spent five years researching, coaching, teaching, implementing and learning from some incredibly powerful people in our industry, and I am sharing everything I have learned. I also have the honour of sharing some incredible success stories from our Team at *Knighton Real Estate Advisors.*

One of the most important things I want to express is the importance of culture and communication with your Empire builder. Empowering and sharing your vision creates a powerful environment for those in your inner circle.

I went right to the basics with Empire Builders and I hope it creates opportunity for those of us in our roles who want to grow into Empire Builders. I hope it provides insight on how to Get Started or Rebuild, if needed.

We will never have perfect systems and we will always be growing. Empire Builders is a guide to help you build systems and models for a successful Real Estate Business and, more importantly, build Empire Builders.

I will leave you with this one message that I hope, after reading Empire Builders, hits home when it comes to building: "Culture always Wins."

CHAPTER 1

WELCOME

Welcome Empire Builders

Here it is; the big opening letter to my book. The part where I'm going to tell you all the amazing things about being an Executive Assistant, an Operations Manager, an Assistant Manager, an Assistant—heck, even an Assistant to the Regional Manager (if you are an office fan, you will get it) in Real Estate.

This is going to be an important book for some of you. And, for some of you, it may contain things you've already heard a million times over, and that's okay. My book is going to be a gentle reminder that you must start somewhere. This book discusses the very fundamentals of systems and models within a high functioning Real Estate team. You are ultimately responsible for what you take away from this book, but I certainly hope there are a lot of great things you will take away from it.

After five years in the Real Estate industry working with some of the best Real Estate Agents you could ever imagine, I was given the opportunity to empower, educate, train, and mentor Administrators (Admins) and some of the best Real Estate Assistants in Canada. So, I have decided it's time to start sharing my knowledge with others. I've had the opportunity to be a part of a highly successful Real Estate team, in Ontario, and one of the things I've always wanted to make sure of is that I give back. I'm sharing my success story with you in hopes that it'll help overcome any obstacles you may be experiencing, as you grow your own business, and help eliminate some of the hiccups to get there.

I want to set us both up for what's coming. I'm going to share a lot of value in this book. Each chapter will be filled with a foundational moment for each part of your Real Estate business. I'm going to talk about the database. I'm going to talk about accountability. I'm going to talk about communication systems and models. I have written this book to empower Agents and Admins to understand how important working together is for your Real Estate business. I will not only share these systems with you; I'm going to teach you from the basics how to build it up. I want to have you walk through the process of putting these systems into place. And, more importantly, I can't wait to hear your success stories.

Being in the Administrative world for five years, now, has taught me one thing: Administrators need to stick together. When you have the right community and the right culture around you, you can take this job and build it into a career, and I'm living proof of that. In this book, we're going to learn some secret formulas to a successful Real Estate career and running a million-dollar Real Estate office team. I'm going to share my struggles and my successes, all of which I am very proud of.

I want to walk with you through this book because if you picked it up, and if you've bought it, you're interested in knowing how to be better at your job. More importantly, if you've bought this book out of your own free will, it tells me you want more out of your job. You want to make it a career, and this book will help you get there.

Five years ago, I left the banking industry after deciding to make a career change. I loved the people I was working with. I loved being in the bank. But, one thing I couldn't grasp was the change in how we serviced our clients. We started to be more product-based than relationship-based. For me, I built my business through relationships, so I started to think long term and what was best for me. I'm not motivated by money; I'm motivated by helping others. I knew I wouldn't be happy at the bank if we continued to treat our customers as products. So, I got comfortable being uncomfortable and started putting my resumes out in the Real Estate industry. I knew that my next move needed to be my last because I have a family and cannot keep running to find happiness within my career. I had to be purposeful with my career hunt. I knew that I wanted to be part of the Real Estate industry and I had a huge desire to learn more around the day-to-day operations... I love that. I knew that I needed to be in a place that allowed me to be creative and build a business within a business. It was very important to me that, during my search, I looked for careers that gave me the opportunity to grow and so I applied to only Real Estate postings. Within a few days, I received a call from a brokerage that, at the time, was brand new to Canada.

I interviewed with a wonderful lady who set me up with an Agent who was looking to hire his very first Executive Assistant. Through the entire process, I was waiting for the doubt to kick in—the regret of leaving my bank job, all of the mixed emotions and, surprisingly, I didn't have any of that. I was filled with excitement of what's to come. The Agent shared his vision of his business and I knew it just felt right.

I'm just going to back up for a minute and go back to when we first met. I met with this Agent, who was looking for his first Executive Assistant, and he was on the cusp of having a stellar year. One of the golden rules, and you'll hear it in my book again, is that knowing when to hire your Admin can be life-changing to your career. We spoke about vision and growth, and there really wasn't much spoken about actual Real Estate and the role. We just talked about where we wanted to go. The conversation quickly became a team convo. It became our vision. I accepted the job, and that's exactly what it was for literally three days. That is all it took for me to realize this is something I can build. I can create systems around his goals.

Don't worry! If you are reading this and think that sounded easy, it was, and I am prepared to show you how it can be an easy decision for you too. I dedicated a whole chapter in this book on knowing when to hire and how hiring the right Admin will double your business. I want to point out that it was the best career move for me and I have never looked back.

For a long time, we hit the ground running as a strong team of two. We then hired our first Buyer Agent and, within the last four years, our tiny team grew from there to become a team of fourteen strong.

During my third month with our team, I went to California to attend training for Assistants that was hosted by a highly successful Real Estate Agent. I sat in this class surrounded by a room full of Admins, all eager to learn systems to grow a team. The room's energy was incredible. I absorbed every inch of what this lady had to say because it fit exactly with what I wanted to do. Not only did it educate me, but it also empowered me and I will forever be grateful for how she inspired me.

How many Admins right now are reading this and feel like they are just in a job? What if I told you that you have an opportunity right now to change the way you've looked at things and to change the way you treat your role? More importantly, what if I told you I am going to empower you in this book to become one of the highest-level Admins in the industry? And, even more importantly, the secret weapon in Real Estate.

Throughout my five years in this role, I have grown from Executive Assistant to Director of Operations for our team. I eventually started my own coaching company, where I coach

Admins and Agents, and I realized this is exactly where I want to be. The lack of coaching, training, and mentoring for Admins led me to go down this path to create systems and create the foundation for successful Real Estate teams. I jumped through the hoops, so you don't have to. How can I not share this with you?

Throughout this book, I am going to switch titles. I might say Executive Assistant, Admin, or Operations. You will see me use different expressions for the role. The reality of it is that it is all the same role.

At this point, I have not even introduced myself. My name is Valerie, and I'm the Director of Operations for a fast-growing Real Estate team. I am also a Real Estate Coach for a lot of teams in Canada, and in the U.S. I honestly believe that we are the secret weapon in Real Estate.

I write this book in two simple formats. One format speaks to the Agent, because I strongly believe in systems and I believe in sharing everything, successfully, in hopes that we can create a massive environment of like-minded individuals in the Real Estate industry. The second format speaks to the Admins trying to build something amazing for the team, and for you, while building a legacy. I am giving you my vision of what life is like in the world of an Admin. I will break this down here so you can read the book and fully understand why it's written the way it is.

To the Agent, please read this as the role of the visionary because a lot of the time I will speak to you in regard to the company's visions, systems and models, and share basic foundational steps to get you to a high level, so that you understand

and appreciate why an Admin is so important to your business and building future Empire Builders. I hope that you are what we call the "integrator," after reading this book. You take the vision the Agent has, and you make it happen.

Both Agents and Admins need to understand your roles for the solid growth of your business. You might even ask, "Why do I strongly believe in the foundation?" That is a great question. Just keep reading. This book will unlock the basic steps to start growing your Real Estate team. I'll share my own team's successes and failures throughout the book because we've had to make mistakes to learn. We've made our share and we've learned a lot.

After a successful year of coaching, I realized one common thing: Admins do not know their worth. We are typically hired and told we're there to do paperwork. That's what you see on most job descriptions. I'm here to show Admins everywhere that we are way more than that, and I'm living proof that you can build a fantastic career in Real Estate. Finding the right Admin can be difficult. Hiring Top Talent can be time-consuming. It can take you from your business. And, we all know that in Real Estate you need to be on your game. Don't worry! I've got your back because the whole chapter is dedicated to hiring and retaining Top Talent, regardless of if this is your first hire or your tenth. Stick to the basics!

Here is a personal message I want to send to all Assistants, Directors of Operations, or whatever your title may be. I'm writing this book for you. I'm writing this book because I want you to realize one thing; if this is the job for you, keep reading this book. It will show you how you can build a business for your Real Estate Agent and become the Empire Builder you want to be. This book will show you exactly what systems you need to build a successful Real Estate team and it will give you the mindset to think like a CEO. It's the Admin to CEO mindset.

The benefits of this book are enormous. Each chapter will guide you through an effective system and give you the knowledge to build up the model and tailor them to your own business. Many Admins out there want more. We have a love for Real Estate, and we want to make a sustainable business for ourselves and our Agents. I want to empower you both to know that you can create a career within this world. I hope this book is in every brokerage's hands. Imagine the power you've just given your Agents by giving them this book. You're empowering the Agent, to find Top Talent and let them partner with them to build a business. The ripple effect this can have on our industry is undeniable.

This book holds the tools to the basic knowledge in Real Estate. Your Agents can leverage their business by hiring a secret weapon or rebuilding the relationship they currently have with their Admin. This book can train them to get to a high level in Real Estate, faster than starting from scratch.

What is coming up in this book is the ability to create and empower your Admins to build high-level systems and models that will take you to the next level. If these models and systems are followed, you will be setting the path for increasing your revenue. It won't be easy, and it will require an entrepreneurial mindset and a strong foundation of communication between Agents and Admins, but the possibilities are endless.

How am I going to keep this promise to you? By the end of this book, you will implement an effective listing system and build a CRM with a strong follow-up. You will either have, or be, a secret weapon with the confidence to run a million-dollar Real Estate team using this method. Whether you are a single Agent or a team, you will be able to build systems. This book will teach you how to build a system for growth, but not for your current situation. I always tell the Admins that I'm coaching, "You never build a system for your current team members. You build it so you are ready to grow." There is already space for growth. Think big and aim big. You will be the ultimate Empire Builder.

Here is what you will need as you read this book:

- An open mind
- The desire to grow a business with your Admins
- Admins, the "want" to build a career
- Pen and paper to take notes, or a highlighter to highlight as you go

Here is what you won't see, and something that's so hard to NOT do...and that is smiley faces. I love a good smiley face. I am hoping you can feel my happiness at the end of every chapter...or paragraph.

For the sake of anyone wondering what sort of value I can bring you, I will share some of our team's stats, at the time I wrote this book:

- Top 1 percent within our Real Estate Board
- Top 3 in Canada within our company

- Top 7 in all teams in our city throughout all Brokerages
- Top 2 in our Brokerage

We continue pushing forward using this very method I am sharing.

CHAPTER 2

HIRING TOP TALENT

and Building a Partnership

O ne of the things we are famous for is turnover in Admin world. How many of us have hired an Admin and they didn't last ninety days? I want to work through that. I want us to admit that sometimes it is because we are not set up to hire, and we don't know what an Admin is supposed to do. There is nothing wrong if you are shaking your head yes to that. Sometimes we blame the lack of progress on the new hire, and sometimes this is the case, but it also has a lot to do with us—the ones doing the hiring. Lack of systems and resources can make it hard to train and build a role. I think what you need to understand is that you are taking away precious time from your clients and your business every time you hire and fire.

One important thing to do is to know when it is time to hire an Admin (many people have mixed answers to this). My rule on when to hire an Admin is simple. It's when you simply cannot keep all the balls in the air. This is typically around the twenty-five-deal mark. Your paperwork is not living up to standards, you are not calling your clients back on time, and you are losing out on potential business because you can't get to lead-generating. You're either not time blocking for success OR you are ready to hire your Empire Builder—let's go with the latter. I like to say it's time to hire when you hit the twenty-five-deal mark and have three months-worth of salary in the bank account. That is a good time to start seeking talent.

The golden rule of hiring is *don't* hire to fill a need. Take the time and hire Top Talent, so you never have to worry about hiring again. Use hiring websites to put your ad out there. Indeed, social media and LinkedIn have been some great resources for my team, or recruit actively by looking at the people you run into. Coffee shop cashiers, Administrators right out of college (connect with your local post-secondary schools). Also, ask other Agents in your office, who have just gone through hiring, if they had any potential candidates that you could interview.

When you are ready to move forward and start the interviewing process, here are some key points to be aware of:

Do not settle; if something in your belly tells you this does not feel right, it is usually correct. Do not let just anyone run your business. What to seek; someone with a business mindset, entrepreneurial mindset, positivity, self-motivated, great family life, etc. Check their social media; how they behave online is important because they are a reflection of *you* and your growing business.

Hire someone who can talk to your clients like you do, or BETTER! The person who fills those shoes must be prepared to build an empire, and a career worth having. A successful hire will double your sales in a year. You will go from twenty-five to forty deals with the right Empire Builder. A lot of the time, people forget what they are looking for because they are wrapped up in how much an Admin will cost them, what to pay an Admin, and do they get bonuses?

I have built a strong Admin team on salary, one-week vacation in the first year, and an incentive plan for them so on their first day there is no confusion around salary, vacation, and so on. Look to your local market to see what the average Admin is paid in your area. Typically, it is around $35,000–$45,000 with bonuses paid out every quarter, in our area.

All right, so we've gone through the hiring process and you found your Empire Builder. You've hired your Top Talent, and it's day one. What are you going to do? How have you set everybody up? You're probably in panic mode because, let's be honest, your specialty isn't hiring and training and it's certainly not administrative work. As a Real Estate Agent, you never get into Real Estate because the paperwork is fun. Now, some of you excel at paperwork and are amazing at it. Ultimately, however, you can't be crushing Real Estate deals and doing paperwork on the back end. That's where we, the Admins, come in. That's where we take over and that's where we create the systems and models to take you forward in your business.

So, you're probably in panic mode and you're not 100 percent prepared on how you want to build your business. The first real system to have in place, once you have hired, is the famous 30/60/90 system. If, at this moment, you read this and you're like, "What the heck is 30/60/90?" don't panic; I got you! To set up your new Admin for success they need to know what their daily tasks are for the first few weeks, this gives you an opportunity to understand daily expectations. This system will give your new Admin guidance on what the next thirty days will look like, what jobs you need them to do, and what methods they need to get started on. We will also be touching on the 80/20 system. It's so important to include this method, as well. I hope I haven't lost you just yet. We will cover all of this, I promise!

What are your weaknesses? Where do you need your Admin to step in and support you? More importantly, what can they do on this day, right now, to help you take care of all this stuff you couldn't do for weeks? What you do from there is build your 30/60/90. The first thirty days is getting familiar with current systems, getting comfortable around Real Estate transactions and understanding the paperwork. If you are confused about 30/60/90, ask other Real Estate Agents in your office who already have an Administrative team to show you theirs.

Some people might call it one hundred days, which is one hundred days of training or training operations manual. There are a lot of different words for it. The reality of it is leverage, and the whole reason you are hiring somebody is that you need that leverage. So don't be afraid to seek outside support on your growth, individually or with an Admin, to help you around the initial starting point.

There are a lot of resources out there. Get a coach. If you already have a business coach, find an Administrative coach who can work with you on your vision, plans, and goals. Give support to your new Admin. Seek another Admin in your office and see if they can shadow one another.

As we go through this part of the book, we will talk about a few systems to implement right away that will help you. Right off the bat, you know what your 30/60/90 is going to look like. You know what you want from your Admin on day one. We'll set you both up for success. If you are still struggling with this, find yourself a coach. I just touched on this briefly above, but seriously hire a coach who will hold you accountable to your goals. Once you hire the Admin, get them a coach. It's important to understand the power of support, not just in hiring an Admin but also in providing training and support for the Admin. More importantly, work with someone who's done this, who's perfected systems that have run successful Real Estate teams. Someone who really knows their stuff! That person is going to teach your Admin everything they need to know to push your business forward. It's a huge support and there's a huge need for it. So, let's get started. Let's get you set up for success!

The next few paragraphs will prepare you for what comes next, and there are many systems out there around this. This is what works for our team, and I use this for every hire. Let's go back to the 30/60/90. We created a 30/60/90 that is broken down into months and after every thirty days we review. If you start your hiring process being completely open and honest, you are setting yourself up for successful on-boarding. During the process, create the environment that if this is not working out, let's talk about it. At the end of every thirty days, you want to ask two questions: How have the first thirty days been for you? What could we be doing better? And then the bonus questions: How do you think you are doing? What did you learn in the first thirty days? *Listen* to their answers— they are building your hiring process as they speak. Let them communicate with you. At the end of the ninety days, you sign a new contract (or a commitment, as I call it) with all the final details as the probation period comes to an end.

Communication for Success After the On-Boarding

After setting them up with a 30/60/90 outline, set up your foundation. Communication is the key to a successful on-boarding. How do you want to be communicated with? Our team chooses the end of day email during the first days of hire. At the end of every day, the Admin commits to sending an email with the following questions: What did I do today? What were my struggles/challenges? How did I overcome them? Do you have any questions? Do you need anything? This is critical. Please read this email and make sure you listen to what they are saying. Going into the next day, you are prepared to help them with any challenges. It will also fill the gaps that are needed in the training process.

With a strong 30/60/90 system, you will not need to stress over the training. Each thirty days, outline specifically what you need from them. Stay the course with them throughout. During the full ninety days, you will work together and form a strong bond. It will be messy, and there will be times you are too busy to communicate. Utilize the end-of-day email method to continue building your foundation. Foundation and structure are the beginnings of a great relationship with your Empire Builder.

Building a Business Together

When you hire your first Admin, you both want to build trust. Why? Because this person is going to be your voice when you cannot be present. They will build trust with your clients for you... FOR YOU! They will also be a part of your finances, so you must trust that person. Let them know how you work with your clients to provide the same, if not *better*, service to your clients. Your Admin will talk to your database, follow-up with your clients, check-in on those you haven't been able to connect with, and continue to build a rapport for the business, so it's important they understand you and how you treat others.

Pop Quiz

I am asking this question to you both Agent and Admin. If you were in a car together, who would be driving? Stop and think about the answer—do not just read to get to the answer. If you are both reading this book simultaneously, I want you to reach out to each other with that question and see what the answer is. If you both said your Admin is driving, you are correct. To be fair, there are no wrong answers, but typically your Admin is driving. You trust them to drive the car. This is the car that will get you to point A, whatever you make point A be. You have the location and they need to figure out the best route to get you there. Now, I'm not saying get in a car and do this. I'm speaking metaphorically, of course. Building trust will not happen overnight. You must work on it. Now, you may get off-track from time to time, and that is okay. Don't stress! They have brought water and healthy snacks for the ride, and they will get you there. This one will be hard to understand, initially, but after you read this book it will all make sense.

After they are established in their role, find out their goals. The Admin has probably changed since you hired them. Find out how you can help them. You are building culture for long-term growth for the two of you. Sounds silly, I bet, but it isn't. I guarantee that when you allow your Admin to talk about growth and vision, it will be the rocket fuel to your business. Letting them know just how important they are to your business will empower them to build it with you. It's amazing what the power of opportunity in the workplace can do.

What Kind of Leader Will You Be?

There is a difference between a leader and a boss, and you can decide which one you will choose to be. Leading by example is extremely important, especially if you ask your team to mirror your clients' behaviour. How you treat others is seen and heard, and speaks volumes about what type of leader you are.

Definition of a Leader: A leader can see how things can be improved and rallies people to move toward that better vision. Leaders can work toward making their vision a reality whilst putting people first. Just being able to motivate people isn't enough—leaders need to be empathetic and connect with people to be successful.

Definition of a Boss: A person who employs, or superintends, workers; manager. A person who makes decisions, exercises authority, and dominates.

The definition of both titles is different, and when reading them, one sounds like someone you want to work with and the other sounds like someone you work for. Just because it's a Real Estate industry doesn't mean you can't build a reputable business. As an example, in all my years on our Real Estate team, I've been in charge of hiring, training, recruiting, creating 30/60/90 for our Administrative team, and many other teams within our market centre. It's probably one of my favourite things to do. Because of that, I am happy to say that my turnover rate is at 1 percent. I lost one Admin since we started implementing structure. The only reason why I lost her was because her husband got a job in California, and she decided to up and move. She is welcome back on our team anytime; I will always have a spot for her. But we lost her due to that, not because of systems, not because of models, not because of leadership. I feel strongly when it comes to turnover and knowing the reasons behind it.

People leave jobs because of their bosses. How you show up early as a leader, and leading by example, will be the biggest asset to your business. As a leader, you show up every day, and showing up includes your words, actions, and how you treat others. Believe it or not, your Admin is watching what you do. First off, they want to make sure they hear how you communicate to clients so they can communicate just the same as you would. So, we watch for that stuff. We watch for culture because chances are we've left an industry that we didn't want to be part of due to a lack of culture, a lack of communication, a lack of trust, a lack of excitement, and so on. Learn why, or learn what, makes them happy and what motivates them. That is how you communicate.

I'm never prepared to let go of the client's experience. I will always make sure every person on our team delivers top-notch client experience, or they are terminated just based on that alone. I have zero tolerance for negativity around our clients. Our clients are one of the most important things to us, they trust us and I will make sure we deliver on that trust every day.

Sorry, I got off topic there. I feel very passionate about the client experience. It's all how we approach and tell people what to do, getting the job done, treating people like they're equal partners, like you are on the same page. This elevates, motivates, and inspires something in all of us to want more and to do better. That's the kind of environment you need to create with your Admin.

The one thing I will always express to you is the "Yes, how?" mentality, and how by having that attitude you will win every single time. Not a "No, how?" mentality, but always a

"Yes, how?" mentality. I can do that, and here is how I am going to do it. A lot of us can have this "No" mentality and that does not get you anywhere. As an Admin, our job is to support our Agents with what they're not capable of doing, taking their ideas and creating something from their vision.

When an Agent comes in, bless their hearts, they're like flying squirrels. They come in with a thousand ideas and they want everything done in fifteen seconds. It is how we communicate back that's important. *Yes, that's a great idea. I got this. Here is how I'm going to do it. Here is when it's going to get done.* Notice that there is no negativity or questioning. This is key for all of us as we build our relationships together.

Agents, I didn't forget about you, my flying squirrels, you need to understand that we can't get everything done in fifteen seconds, and it hurts my heart to say that to you. We are not machines. One day, there will be an Admin who can complete tasks in fifteen seconds, but we are not there yet, so I kindly ask you, on behalf of all Real Estate Admins, when you have a large to-do list, understand they're going to take that list, prioritize it, and get it done. If you use all the methods that I am teaching you in this book, you will have strong communication about how and when your to-do lists will get done.

People who don't work well under pressure; talk to us. We are working with you here. We are partners in this. We're here for you. Do not set us up for failure because we cannot communicate properly. Be the leader you want the Admin to be. One super important thing is *Admin goals,* when you find that hire. That Top Talent Administrator. Find out what their goals are in life. Find out where they see themselves in the future.

They want things as well, such as a trip, a renovation project, a savings account, a goal of making a specific amount of money. Find out what their goal is and help them get there. You're in an industry where you can help create wealth for others. They will be an asset to their company's growth. Know their goals, desires, and financial goals. Let them track their goals. Let them have a growth plan from within the team. You might have an Admin whose goal is to get their Real Estate licence in a year. Imagine if you can help that person get there.

Your job is to know their plans, goals, and big "whys," because their vision is now part of your big vision, as I talked about at the beginning. Coming from someone in the Admin world, it feels good that people want to hear about us and that we are not just that person at a desk answering phone calls. If that is the type of Admin you want, I will be honest with you; this book is not for you. This is a book about how an Admin and an Agent can work together to build a strong relationship. Better yet, build a big foundation for an amazing Real Estate business.

It is your job, Agents, to know your Admins' goals. They become your family. They will work with you more than they will see their own family; and same goes for you. So, treat them like family and you will always have a great relationship.

CHAPTER 3

GOAL PLANNING

O ne of the things I think is extremely important to express here, as we go into chapter three, is the need for vision. You probably already have a vision. That's the reason you're at the next stage and are hiring an Administrator, which is great. Now, sit down and think about your long-term vision. You will have to start asking yourself what kind of wealth you are creating for yourself, your Admin, and your family. What kind of life are you going to live because of what you are doing as you build something big? That is really what this chapter is all about. It's laser-focused on not the moment you're in right now but setting yourself up for future success.

What if you were to say something worded completely different? To say something in a way that makes someone feel the value in that role. I think that is the most important thing when hiring an Administrator. Anyone can say, "I'm just going to need you to file paperwork. Make sure it's complete and stamp a few envelopes." But what if you told them that they would be handling all the relationships between the clients and the brokerage? What have you told them about your vision? Once you establish all this, you are on this journey together. It is not just you. It opens the doors and expands your minds to think so much bigger on this.

At this point, you might be reading this and thinking, *Why are we going to all this trouble to build a business? I just want to do deals and help clients.* That is certainly an option. There is nothing wrong with that. If that is what you want to do, then take a few bits and pieces, tips and tricks, from this book and build just that. What I am telling you is that, from my own experience, you can take this role into a career. Double your business and help more people fulfill their dream of homeownership. It can be so much bigger than you might think.

Imagine you get to the point in your career where you've reached a high level of success, and you can start giving back to the community. That's where my team is at right now. That's why I need to help the next level of Admins and/or Agents coming into this industry. I think it's super important that we understand that the relationship between the Admin and the Agent is the most important thing from the very beginning. We are your secret weapon because you have given us this opportunity. We want nothing more than to help grow your business.

Let's get started talking about vision and goal planning, and all the fun stuff to push you and your Admin forward into next year, and into the future, so that way when your Admin comes in on day one, or every single day for the next few years, they know exactly what the long-term goal is and what the vision is for you guys as a team. They also know exactly what needs to get done to get there. Imagine creating an environment that felt like Christmas every day; that's a personal goal of mine for our office. I want people to be excited to come to work. It is not just Real Estate. This isn't just about selling homes; it's about helping families. That is what it's all about.

SIDE NOTE: Whether you're in a room together, reading the book at different times, or not reading the book together at all, when you get to a part where I ask questions, I want you to stop and think about it for a minute then process the question in your head. I will be asking a lot of questions that I truly want you to stop reading and think about.

Now, let's get ready to create a vision so big that anybody else who wants to be part of it will fit into it, as well. Are you ready? So, where do you start with goal planning? Most Agents just love doing deals and working with clients. What will separate you from all the average Agents are your goals and visions. Establish concrete goals. Are you ready? I am about to jump into some formulas for goal planning.

Let's take a moment so I can say that you may have come up with a different goal, there is no right or wrong here. We all have different goals in our business. I created a formula that will be extremely helpful for anyone who struggles around goal planning.

Goal Planning Simplified

Units per year (eventually, you will break this number down quarterly). How many new clients to add to the database (eventually you will ask yourself where they will come from)? What's your Average Commission so you can focus on what your GCI is? I'm talking basic goals for now so that those who are just starting to goal plan have a great foundation. Once you've established your goals, share them with your Admin or, better yet, work on them together so you can both share the vision and achieve those goals. Putting a plan in place to get you there is what us Empire Builders do!

I'm going to backtrack for just a second because some of you are wondering how we got here. Before you can determine a basic foundation for your growth, there are certain questions you need to ask yourself. Ask yourself these additional questions: The answers to these questions will help with budget and financial planning if you are looking to build a team.

How much money do I want to make this year?

How many families do I want to help?

How much money do I *need* to make this year to keep the lights on?

Now, let's focus on the first list of goals. I will use even numbers with the following formulas to help make it easier to understand. Goal: $100,000 this year. How do you get there? Take your Average Commission; let's say it is $10,000 (this is after splits). So, $10,000 x number of homes you need to sell = 10 (you will need to do ten deals to meet your GCI goal). There is your unit goal and your GCI goal. Some of us have some great formulas around this, but this is ideally a simple start to building out your goals.

Now you have hired an Admin—your Empire Builder—and you have the additional overhead. Are your expenses included in that $100,000? Let's assume salary and overhead = $66,000. Add it to your $100,000 (that $100,000 is just for you). That's $166,000, which means $66,000 to keep the lights on and salary for your growing business. Now you need to project Average Commission x Units you need to sell to get to $166,000.

You are creating your goal. It is going to sound scary, and you may doubt if you can attain it. I'm telling you right now that if you have aligned yourself with Top Talent, they will help you get there. This is where leverage comes in. Below, I will give you a basic formula for focusing on goals and how you can leverage your Empire Builder to build this with you. There will be additional layers of goals as you build, but establishing the foundation is a must.

Your units will now become how many families you intend to help. See what I did there! Let's say you want to help forty families this year. How do you do that? Ask the question, how do we help forty families this year with their homeownership goal, and how committed are we to this vision? Don't skip to the formula just yet; I want you guys to be asking each other these questions, whether you are in a room together or having to text one another. It doesn't matter if you are not reading this simultaneously; you will understand and push each other to have a high level of conversations.

Here is my formula. I'm sharing it early in the book and will break it down throughout the book for you. This formula is called the 80/20 rule. Pareto's Law to some, and a very popular formula for Real Estate. Over the years, I have taken this formula and broken it down into a system (as Empire Builders usually do). I created a way for Admins to understand the importance of the Agents' top 20 percent. We were hired to take over the things the Agents are not good at or don't have the time to do to the best of their abilities. So above you've established monetary goals, and now you have to determine how you will get there. What are the additional goals within the team to work on? What will you focus on and what will they focus on? Then build out from there to help achieve those goals.

Secret Formula

Frequently, I get asked, "How does our Admin know what system to build?" A lot of Admins will ask, "Where do I start?" Therefore, this chapter is really about laying the foundation. We've spoken about the vision and the importance of having a vision for your team, and sharing the vision. We spoke briefly about the secret formula. It took me about two years in the Real Estate industry to realize what that secret formula was. A lot of us go to training workshops, and it is like drinking from a water hose. Everyone's telling you where to start. Your Agents are giving you a list of things that they want to be done. There's no ultimate training or system building. Every day, you're just fulfilling a task list. That is just a method to get you through the day. It isn't a sustainable system, and it's not going to get you to success. It's just mediocrity, just grinding it out with your to-do list.

About two years into the role, I realized that there must be a better way to help Admins understand what systems their Agent needs; there has to be a better way to know where to start building, and that is how I got to this formula. Ask yourself, and them, "What is their job and what is my job?" I think that is a big thing right there, in itself.

This secret formula is the basic system for the Admin and the Agent on how to get started, and who does what. Agents, I want you to grab a pen right now. Admins, you as well. We are going to do a quick little question period. Agents, I want you to write down your top six jobs. Go ahead . . . I'll wait. Administrators, I want you to write down what you think the Agent's top six jobs are. Now, what I'm going to do next is just let you know that there're no wrong answers. I'm just using a formula that works for our team and has been one of my key pieces when I coach new Admins during on-boarding. You will take your answers, and you will build from there. I'll explain more in a minute.

I can't take credit for the next six things that I'm about to share with you. This is what our team focuses on. This is what I coach all Admins when I talk about the 80/20 rule. What I did do, is take this formula that most Real Estate Agents use and created a system around it to help Admins understand what the 80 percent means, and how to support the 20 percent. This is my formula, formed from Pareto's Law, where 20 percent of your actions yield 80 percent results. I look at it this way; 20 percent is your Agent's top 20 percent, and everything else is your Admin, so the Admin gets the 80 percent. Now we must identify what that 20 percent looks like. What are your top six jobs? Again, this list that I am about to share with you, I didn't come up with it. I came up with the formula and I build systems using what I am about to share.

Did you answer the questions I asked above? I want you and your Admin to compare notes. Before I give you my answers, I would love to see the two of you compare notes on that. Hang on to those notes. Remember, there are no wrong answers. On our team, our Agents' top 20 percent are the following:

1. Going on appointments
2. Lead-generation
3. Follow-ups
4. Negotiating contracts
5. Networking
6. Tracking numbers

This list is not in any particular order. If you did not hit any of those six, that's okay. If you want to change what is on your list, that's okay too. What you will do now is sit down with your Admin and go through that list.

You are going to take number one, and again, just for the sake of having something to go off of, I'm going to go off my list. So, number one is going on appointments. From there, your Admin will now create the system around that. Example: Using a Google calendar for both of you. Your Admin invites you to that appointment with the client's contact information and the address of that appointment in the note section. Then so on, and so on, and you build a system out from that.

Follow-up is another top job. Example: Is it to ensure that you have a top-of-the-line CRM that allows you to have reminders and notes, so you constantly receive notifications of your follow-up calls? Use the Google calendar to time block yourself when you focus on follow-ups using whatever system you have in place.

What is the system around lead-generation? Is it a calendar and time block time that you will be lead-generating? How are you protecting your time? What happens when the lead or appointments are booked? I'm trying to say this formula will help build systems for your Agent's top 20 percent. It's going to need support. As an Admin, you take that 20 percent and you build your formula, or systems, from that. You can also Google "Pareto's Law," to understand the basics of it. It does not have anything to do with Real Estate and yet it can be applied to almost everything we do. When I coach Administrators, I always use this formula and I start by asking the same question: What're your Agent's top six jobs? Here is the thing I think is important to mention: You might not have six jobs, and that's okay. Pick the top 20 percent of your items that you want to focus on, and everything else is your Admins. *Agents*, you need to be okay with that. You need to give up that control on that 80 percent so your Admin can take that and build something incredible. That is the secret right there on starting systems and knowing where to get started. You have to have good communication skills to get to this point. What I've done is I've allowed you all to forego the small steps and jump right into where you can start building your system.

Quick Review of the Secret Formula:

Agents Top 20 Percent
- Lead-generation – How many contacts go into the database?
- Follow-up – Call your follow-ups DAILY
- Negotiating contracts
- Going on appointments
- Networking – Building a sphere
- Tracking numbers – Analyze and you hold yourself accountable.

80/20 RULE

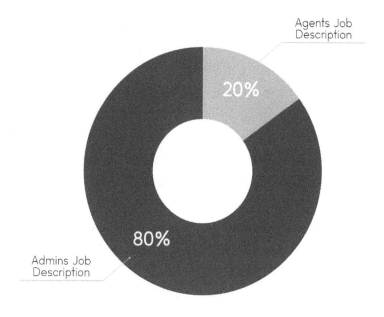

Agents Job Description

20%

Admins Job Description

80%

What will your 80% be?

To my Empire Builders: Take those top six jobs and build systems from them. Below, I go into more detail about how you can support your Agent and their 20 percent.

Lead-Generation: What system will they use to lead-generate? Cold-calling? How will you protect their time to allow them to lead-generate? Take their cell phone and give them a landline to avoid distractions. Time block two hours a day to focus on lead-generation.

Follow-Ups: A great CRM will help. It will help you to set you up reminders to call your clients who are in your follow-ups. Time block when they do follow-ups. Make sure they complete those follow-ups. Admins find a great CRM system with templates and calendars to help create a successful follow-up system. The gold is in the follow-ups. We will do a chapter on database management, so don't feel overwhelmed at this moment.

Negotiating Contracts: This is an easy one. Admins, you make sure contracts are in place and the client has all the details of contracts ready, so the Agent only has to research offers and negotiate on the client's behalf. This is something we can also work on outside of this book.

Going on Appointments: As an Admin, we often don't realize how much help we actually can be for our Buyer Agents: pulling the map, booking showings, preparing the home sheets for the buyers.

Networking: Where does your Agent need to be? What groups should they be part of? How will you get them there? Delegate a set amount of time each month to get your Agent in front of people outside of their social calendar. Is there a high-level networking event they should be at, or a charity event or other community event to be involved in? Look for these things and get them there.

Tracking Numbers: How do you support this? Know the numbers. Have your own goal in place on how you will help them achieve those numbers. Have a tracking sheet (Excel or Google) where they can be tracked and shared. Have a huge whiteboard in their office with goals written out. Talk about those numbers. Every Monday, share the prior week concerning your goals.

Know the Numbers: Have a planner for your team to write out yearly, monthly, weekly, and daily goals. This will set you apart from the average Admin. It takes some Admins years to get to this point, and if you can take the above and build out systems to help your Agent grow, you will surpass all others in the industry. This formula alone took me two years to implement and to realize that the 80/20 rule was the best job description I ever needed.

Budget

As we wrap up chapter three, we're going to jump into the last part here, which is Budget. It feels like we're all over the place, so why in chapter three are we talking about the budget when we are talking about the vision and the goal? As you grow, and when I say this, I mean from Agent with an Admin to Agent and small team, you will need to start with a budget, tracking income and expenses. It's a whole book in itself and I'm not going to take a lot of time going over budget, expenses, and income because, to be honest with you, I'll probably lose you in this book. Instead, I'm going to give you the basic foundation to get started with your accounting for the team.

As an Admin, we should be performing this role ourselves. Again, it is one of those things where it's not in the job description. It is just another hat that we're wearing, and that is okay! Trust me, I've been there and I've mastered this because I simply didn't have a choice. When I started with our team, it was just my team leader and I, and he needed someone to do our accounting, tracking expenses, and collecting receipts. If you're an Agent without an Admin right now, this should help you get started.

I highly recommend using QuickBooks. Go to www. quickbooks.ca and create an online account, so you get a cloud account. A cloud account allows you to access Quick-Books from your phone or desktop. You can take it with you. You can access it and share it with your accountant, which is extremely valuable. This was a game-changer for me. What you want to do with your budget is to know what you need to track. I can give you six good things to track, and again, I'll show you how. We will talk a little bit more about each one, in this chapter.

There are some typical expenses to track for a realtor. One such expense will be salary, if you have an Admin. Knowing what your office expenses are is very important. If you often sign up for training events and go away for training, make sure you document that. It's really important to know the typical expenses and why it's important to track them. Keep those receipts. It's going to be part of your goal.

As you grow, let's say three years down the line, and you have added another Agent on the team and another Admin, as well. Looking at what your revenue has been for the prior two years is vital. It helps you plan for future growth. Let's just back it up there for a minute; you need to go back and look at your financial records for the past two years, and where you sat for revenue two years ago. It's also a lead indicator of how your business is growing, how fast it's growing, and where your opportunity is to save money. Then it boils down to having the conversations around that.

You can have a P&L (Profit & Loss), but you have to talk about it. Often, the Admin doesn't want to talk to their Agents about the P&L because it's a stress. It's an added stress to the conversation that might not trigger a lovely conversation. No matter how well it's tracked and how great income and expenses are, Agents sometimes just want to go, go, go. When they're being reminded of what they're spending, it's no fun.

I'm going to be quite honest; I fully agree that you, as an Agent, should feel that way. It's not the fun part. It's not fun for us, either. However, it's a conversation that is vital to your relationship with your Admin and it's vital that it's done monthly, and broken down weekly, if possible. On our team, we meet with our Agents on the 15th of every month, and we go over where we are currently at in terms of budget and numbers. Now we have a larger team, so we must sit and have these conversations to know if we're trending on the higher side or the lower side for income and expenses. Then weekly, we have mini touch points to stay on track.

If you're a Real Estate Agent with investments, your Admin should be helping you with your investment portfolio, as well as tracking your rent, property maintenance, and other income expenses. Utilize QuickBooks. Get an Accountant. It took me a good five months until I built a relationship with our accounting firm that we work with now. I work with them more than I work with our team leader. I'm the direct contact for our Accountant. They'll file your taxes, all that kind of stuff needs to get done, and it takes that pressure off your Admin. You need an accountant, anyway, to go through and file all your Year End stuff. Find someone you trust, and who your Admin will get along with, so that they can build a relationship and the only time you need to look at your income and expenses is monthly, to be sure that you're on target.

Tracking salary and tracking marketing budget is an indicator for the next year. This way, you can look back year-to-year and see the amount of money spent on marketing this year compared to last year. You will know if you can expand a little bit and you'll become familiar with what amount is needed for your marketing budget. You can't do that if you're not aware of the expenses from the year before. It's like throwing something to the wall and seeing if it sticks. That's not the method I want you to take when it comes to budget.

I'm going to leave you with a little bit of information about how important it is to have a good budget in place and then one step further; how to communicate it. Just to recap, what I would suggest you do, if you already have a QuickBooks account, is get the online version. Download it and share it with your accountant or invite your accountant to share the iCloud version. Pre-populate your bank accounts and your visa statements, so when your commission cheques are deposited into your account they will automatically go into QuickBooks. Your expenses, your gas, your debit card or visa purchases also go right to QuickBooks, so you can simply pull it up and track it from there. Keep a physical copy of all receipts, and if there're Admins reading this, the best thing that you could do every month, collectively, is put your receipts into individual monthly binders or envelopes and then store them with your Year End filing. It's really important we keep those receipts. Now, I've probably lost a few of you. You've probably skimmed through these last few words because budget, income, and expenses aren't a fun topic. It's fun to see the money flowing in; it's not fun where you see it going out.

You can't grow in your business without knowing what your budget is. You have to protect the income of your team. This can create a long-term goal for you. It does tie into the goals and the visions because you're going to need money to fund all that stuff. So, I'm going to wrap up this chapter and not bore you anymore. I'm always open to questions on how you can do better with it. Good luck with the budget.

A Personal Story: I thought I would share a story with you about why I feel the vision is so important and why sharing the vision with your Administrator is key for growth. Five years ago, when I started this journey, I came from the banking industry. The industry had lost its focus on the client, and we were more focused on how many units we could process, how many people we could say yes to, and how many people we could sign up for credit cards. It just got to a point where we weren't even talking to the client anymore. They were more of a yes/no, approved/not approved entity and I didn't like that.

I'm not afraid to make big decisions. I'm someone who's always had an Administrator working with me and it was amazing. I had so much respect for them because they are the people who get the stuff done behind the scenes. So, I decided to apply elsewhere, and I started thinking that I want a Real Estate career. Real Estate was always something I was interested in, but I just never really took the time to get licensed and go through the process. I started having a family and I started to build a career in banking, and I knew that it was safe. You have your pension and all that stuff that made the job appealing, cushiony, and comforting. It's hard to let that go, but I knew, for me, my passion wasn't about that. It was about always doing the right thing, and I love helping people.

I applied for a job that I noticed on Indeed. It didn't sound too appealing, but I thought I'd give it a try. Something about this ad made me curious. There was no name to the Real Estate company . . . Nothing! I went through the process, and I ended up speaking with one of the brokerage's operating partners. A wonderful lady I can't say enough good things about, and she said, "It sounds to me like you might be a little bit overqualified for this job or just have a little bit more experience, and why would you leave the bank?" That was a great question. I agreed she was right, and I left the interview. Then I thought about it. The way she talked about the company stayed in my mind. I kept going back to the job ad. About four weeks after the initial call, I called her back and said, "You know, I've changed my mind. I want to pursue this to the next step." She agreed and promised the realtor would call me. He was looking for an Executive Assistant, and I would be perfect. I told her to do that. Fifteen minutes later, my team leader, the guy I've been working with for the past five years, called me. We immediately had an interview over the phone, and then another face-to-face interview. Before I could even quit the bank, he had an email address in my name already set up. I started to get all the emails coming through from his business. I was tagged in Real Estate posts on social media, and at that point, I felt I could ask the guy what his problem was, or quit the bank immediately, because he was already so invested in me.

When I say invested, it wasn't money. He saw something in me, and it was that he didn't hire me because he needed somebody. I'm sure people were lining up for this job. He saw something in me and gave me this opportunity. For five years, we've been building one of the most incredible Real Estate teams. The whole point of this story is that we didn't talk about experience or skill when I met with him, or what I could bring to the team. He shared with me his vision, and he asked if I could "handle that." Nothing else mattered. Everything else we'll learn as we go. We'll train each other; we'll help each other get to the next step. I mean, obviously, I said I have to go home and think about it, and that was just the silliest answer because there was no thinking. His vision was so big, and it was exactly where I knew I wanted it to be.

I was validated in my decision that one day he was talking to a client on the phone, just some potential client that he follows up with regularly. She mentioned she was struggling with her garden and she's nowhere near listing her home because her garden was a mess. Her kids couldn't help her, and her husband wasn't able to do so either. Our team leader found somebody to go over to help do her gardening, and he didn't do it because he wanted the listing. He did it because it was the right thing to do. She expressed concern to him while he was talking on the phone. She graciously let him call her. She didn't yell at him. She let him have the conversation, and this was just his way of being grateful; grateful for an opportunity to talk to and help a nice lady.

Did we ever sell her home? I don't have the answer. I don't remember if we ever got a listing from her. But it doesn't matter. That wasn't the point. His vision wasn't to be the best Real Estate Agent with the most units sold. His vision was to help as many people as possible. When we broke that up into individual goals, we focused on what it would look like and how many people the two of us could help. That's when we realized that no matter how big our goal, we would create a team of people to help us help more people.

This sounds a little bit unrealistic in Real Estate because we know our common goal is to sell houses, to get commission cheques and make a lot of money. That's our karma, do the good things in life and this is what comes back. In our five years in business, we've been very fortunate to help over 400 families with homeownership. We started in a small closet office space just the two of us as a team. We are now fourteen people, strong, like-minded individuals who sit down and talk about our team's vision and the direction we're going, every October. When we start a new year, we already have feet on the ground running.

Goal planning is embedded in us daily. We create monthly charts on our goals for the month, and we break those goals down weekly and daily. Our team's success is because we commit every day to goal planning and sharing that same vision of helping others. If you don't have that vision, it won't work out, and that's okay. That's our vision, so we only hire people who are willing to get to that vision with us. If you're reading this and you want that so badly, go back and read this chapter again because that's how you'll get there.

Success Formula Recap for Budgeting
- Get QuickBooks
- Populate everything into QuickBooks
- Have separate bank accounts – make sure the Agent has a business account
- Watch the training video I created on Profit & Loss (P&L) to give you a basic understanding of running a P&L
- Put a budget in place – see the formula below
- Talk about this monthly – I like to call it "Where are we?"

Typical Expenses of a Realtor
- Salaries
- Office Space
- Office Expenses
- Marketing
- Training
- Licensing/Education

CHAPTER 4

LEAD THE WAY

Show Your Value as an Empire Builder

L et's dive into chapter four. One of my favourite things to talk about is how, as an Admin, we can show value to our Agent. What's our ROI? Those of you who don't know what an ROI is, it's the Return on Investment. Our Agents have invested in hiring us. We always want to make sure that we're replacing our salary, and I know that sounds silly to some, but it's true. How do we do that? How do we show our value? I mean, we work hard, we get the job done and we come in every day ready to start and finish off strong. We do those things, but how can we show a true ROI? In my experience, that comes in the form of replacing my salary. In this chapter, we're going to talk about ways that we can build an ROI for the team, and how that ROI can benefit us long-term, as well.

Often, when we go into the room, we sign our job description and we say we're working for this set salary with options for benefits, incentives, and bonuses. I'm the type of person who wants to grow and create my future. I want to create my budget outside of my salary, bonuses, and commissions. How else can I generate additional bonus, or additional income, for myself and our team?

This chapter is dedicated to showing you how you can do that. We're going to talk about how we can utilize our sphere of influence, use our own families and friends, and show them how they can work with our team. What methods we can use to build our brand within the team. We'll do a chapter on branding and marketing, as well. I'm going to give you some great tips and suggestions to help you build your income on top of your salary; how to bring value to the team and replace your salary. Grab a pen and a piece of paper because you're going to want to take notes.

Often, we find ourselves caught up in this notion that we are "just Admins" here to do paperwork and all the dirty jobs the Agents don't want to do. Can we please agree right now to throw that sentence right out the window? If I could delete and rewrite that sentence, I would one hundred times over. This is something I often encounter with our coaching clients. I will be honest; it hurts my heart. To some of you, this may be just a job, a steppingstone, and that's okay. But while you are doing it, remember, it's your legacy, your footprint you leave for the next person. Make it a powerful and deep one!

How can we, as Empire Builders, generate leads for our team and build additional income for ourselves? Well, I have some great tips and suggestions for you.

Social Media: This has two parts and will also be mentioned again in two other chapters in this book. Announce your role to your social media. Change all your info to reflect the team and who you are working with. This way, any friends/family looking for Real Estate knows you are in the industry. Share your team's post (there should be a business page). You can also create videos and share team successes. Create a post and ask, "Do you know anyone looking to buy/sell or invest in Real Estate? If so, send them my way, and I will give you a $25 gift card for your referral." Just to be clear, the gift card is expensed to the team. Message anyone on your accounts who likes or comments immediately. Create your own follow-up system. Ask if they want to be part of your database. Add them to it once they say "yes," and create an email follow-up system so you always stay on top-of-mind and you are not bugging them about Real Estate, all the time.

You are probably wondering, "How do I make additional income from this?" It's simple. Talk to your Agent and ask if you bring in leads to the team, and those leads close, how could that generate additional income for you. If anyone on our Admin team brings a client that we work with and close on, we gift them $500 (bonus to payroll or with a gift card).

Please keep it on the books and document it so that everyone comes out on top of this. Now what you do is you set your goal. How many leads do you want to bring to the team? Develop your plan on how you will get your sphere. Now Agents, if you read this chapter, please make sure that for every lead your Admin brings you, gift them. This is an incentive that will grow your business and help them create more wealth for their future and, more importantly, it is a powerful Return on Investment for YOU!

Introduction to Lead-Generation

Let's just jump right in here. I'm going say "lead-gen" a lot. Some people get extremely uncomfortable when we talk about it. Some Agents want to curl up into a little ball and not want anything to do with it because they associate it with cold-calling and door-knocking. All these activities are so uncomfortable for some people. We, Admins, recognize that. We know it, we hear it, and we get it. We work hard at putting systems in place for you to focus on your lead-gen and nothing else. I've said it before; there are no fires in the Real Estate business that need to be put out immediately. However, every Agent finds a fire right before lead-gen time.

For example, a Real Estate team that I coach are great at getting prepared to lead-gen. Then, it's all about, "Oh, I've got to go get my cup of coffee." "I have to go to the bathroom." "I just got a Facebook notification and I need to check that out." There are no limits to the excuses Agents make for not picking up the phone and making those calls. I've said it before, and I'll say it again, we're not actually in the Real Estate business.

We're in the lead-gen business. I hear this all the time; it's a huge staple for our team. We must wrap our heads around the fact that we've got to lead-gen for business.

Many people think if they get into Real Estate, they'll do deals with friends and family. They believe they have a pipeline of people they went to high school with and that the business will just flow. I think it's safe to say that's not a great way to look at your pipeline. You have to build your pipeline.

I plan to talk to you guys about the database, but I'm building a small foundation so that you'll understand it when we get to the database chapter. We'll talk a little bit about lead-gen, where to put the contacts, and such. We'll touch on it briefly here, and then we'll go into it a little bit more down the road in the database chapter.

What we need to do is learn to be comfortable with being uncomfortable. If you look at your stats from last year, where did you generate the majority of your business? Think about that for a minute, because as you grow this business with your Admin and you add more people to it, you're going to start tracking your lead sources. Lead-gen isn't just about cold-calling. Okay, forget that it's not just picking up the phone and cold-calling people asking them if they're interested in Real Estate. It's a great deal more. You have door-knocking. You have your follow-up calls, marketing, networking, Open Houses, and a lot of other opportunities to generate leads outside of cold-calling.

Here's the thing. If cold-calling scares you, or if it's intimidating or just gives you anxiety, it's probably because you haven't found your groove. Have a purpose and a reason to call somebody and give them value in your phone call. It just doesn't have to be, "Hey, it's 'so and so' from 'so and so.' I'm just checking to see if you're interested in selling your house and/or buying." That's the silliest script ever. Have a purpose when you're making these calls and show them value in those calls. For instance, the Real Estate team that I work with makes their cold-calls to their leads twice a day. A team that I work with in Hamilton spends two hours on lead-gen every Thursday and Friday, cold-calling around their area. If they're hosting an Open House, they call the neighbourhood inviting them to the Open House, allowing them to call with a question and providing value by asking if they have any friends and/or family that are looking to move into the neighbourhood where they are hosting the Open House.

Okay, so that's one example of lead-gen. The second example of lead-gen cold-calling is, "Hey, we just sold a house in your neighbourhood and I just want to know if you are interested in knowing what we sold it for, or if you're interested in listing." That's probably not the best script to use, but I'm just trying to give you an example of another opportunity to bring value to cold-calling. We're going to spend the next little bit talking about some tips and suggestions to get you set up for success and how you can leverage your Administrator to help you.

One of the most important things is protecting your time. Have a set schedule in place when you're going to lead-gen. Make sure your Administrative team knows this. They can take care of all the other stuff on the back end so if anything important comes through, they've got it for you. If you're reading this right now, Administrators get a landline if it's within your budget for your Agent. As you grow a team, make sure everyone has a landline, and here's why: When it comes time to do their cold-calling, take their cell phone because they'll use it as a distraction. There's so much fun stuff in their apps, such as, music, notifications, and whatnot. Take their cell phones; leave them with their laptop and their CRM set up. They can cold-call using the dial phone, or the landline on the desk, and they've got nothing else to focus on but a pen and a piece of paper. Make sure their coffee, or their water, is on their desks for them so they can't use that as an excuse to leave and put a sign on the door that says, "lead-gen happening."

Now, let's talk about accountability. I'm going right into the accountability part, and then you'll see below, we'll break it up into some systems you can use as Admins. Your job is to protect the Agent's time.

Accountability goes back to having goals in place and knowing what you want to attain in a day. How many calls do you want to do? How many people do you want to add to the database? How many people do you want to talk to? Your Administrative team knows this, as well, and they hold you accountable. Write down your goals on a piece of paper. If you're looking to make twenty contacts a day, check off every time you make contact until you get to your twenty. If you reached your contact goal and have added the contacts to the database, you've completed your goal. How many appointments do you want to set? I'm going to tell you a little secret right now; if your goal is to set two appointments a day, you should lead-gen every day from 9:00 a.m. to 11:00 a.m.

When you're done at 11:00 in the morning, and you've set two appointments, you have your entire day ahead of you. You got the hard part out of the way. Some people call it *to eat the frog*: get that part of the day out of the way and the rest of the day is open. Sounds great, doesn't it?

I'm going to just speak to the Admins right now, and please don't hate me for this. It's all for the greater good, and everyone loves accountability. So, Agents cover your eyes. Admins, if you're reading this chapter with your Agent, find out what they lead-gen for and why they are making money. What are they trying to fund in their life? A lavish vacation, a brand-new car, a new house, an investment property? Find out what they want, hang a picture of it, or something similar to it, above their head. Heck, I've even hung my photo above my Agents' head to push them harder, to keep lead-generating when they didn't want to do anymore because they're not just lead-generating for themselves; they are lead-generating for their team. Hold them accountable to that with something visual.

If they come out of that room before their two hours of lead-gen is up, ask if we are one step closer to our goal, or one step farther away, because if you haven't done your twenty contacts and booked your two appointments today, that's four hours of lead-gen tomorrow and now four appointments you need to book. What's it going to look like if we don't book appointments? How will you keep me busy if I don't have any appointments to book for your listings to process? Then show them the flip side. If you book your appointments, and you're going on listing appointments, you now have the whole day to focus on something else.

Let's get started on talking about systems for lead-gen. We're talking the bare minimum, the basic foundation to a good lead-gen system. I'm only scraping the surface because there's so much more to it. Let's dig in and get started on lead-gen systems.

Empire Builders and Agents, here is a system to follow lead-gen and leverage your Admin to increase lead-gen to book appointments. Commit to lead-gen hours. The general rule is two hours a day. Typical lead-gen is cold-calling, social media blasts, and door-knocking. Every week, commit to two hours a day, write it down and tell your Admin those times. Admins, protect those two hours by providing the Agent with a landline instead of a cell phone, and then take the cell phone so there are no distractions. Dedicate those two hours to consistent lead-gen. Nothing on the outside should come in. If you share an office space, shut the door, so there are no interruptions. This is called creating a bunker.

While you are lead-generating, the Admin has everything under control and will deal with clients and other Agents, as things come in. A lot of Agents are afraid to commit to this, so I will share a success story with you. Our team lead-generates for two hours per day, Monday to Wednesday, and it's straight up cold-calling. Thursday and Friday are reserved for door-knocking.

Empire Builder's, it's your job to protect this time because if there's no lead-gen, there's no new business, no pipeline being built, no income coming in. Three months from now you won't be happy with the outcome. Encourage your Agent to push through lead-gen. All they need is a landline, notepad and a laptop with their database. Whatever the method of lead-gen is, put the plan in place to protect this time and help them build a lead-gen system. Script practice with your Agent and find scripting partners for them. We should never be script practicing on our clients. Take your lead-gen to the next level and script practice and role play, especially objections.

Leverage your Empire Builder so that you focus on lead-gen. You are in the lead-gen business, not Real Estate. Think about that for a minute. There are no fires to put out during this time. The energy you put into that day's lead-gen will show up three months from now. Let's say that again, your actions today show up three months from now!

Sunday nights, write out your week. Put it into the calendar and share with your Admin (Google calendar is great for this). Monday through Friday, schedule what your lead-gen hours are, what you are committing to, and what it is you are doing. Monday morning, your Admin comes in, reviews your input, and knows how to protect your time for that week.

I'm going to take this one step further, and you Agents might love me or hate me for this. I hope you love me because I mean it from the bottom of my heart. I give your Admins permission to post what is most important to you above your desk while you lead-gen to keep you reminded why you are doing this. It could be family, your Admin's salary, a vacation; I encourage your Admin to play on your "WHY."

Breakdown the Importance of Lead-Gen for you Both

Empire Builder's, lead-gen and build your book of business. We should be creating opportunities to show our worth and give back. This is called the ROI, and it's important in our industry to always have an ROI on everything we do. What will be your ROI on the team? Start with a plan to promote the team within the industry guidelines to increase brand awareness and generate leads for your team. As an Admin, we can't make a cold-call, so how do we get our team in front of people.

Create a list of twenty people you know that you can add to the database, such as friends and family. Next, create another list of twenty people outside your inner circle and ask yourself, "Do they know I'm in Real Estate?" This list can be full of doctors, lawyers, schoolteachers, etc. Think outside the box.

Once you've established this list, the next time you see these people, let them know what you do. Or call them and let them know. It's your choice on how you want to proceed. Social media is a good market for you and for promoting the team, as well.

Stick to your Lead-Gen Goal

I want to break down the importance of lead-gen for both the Agents and the Admins. It's important to understand how you can lead the way and show your worth with the systems that I just shared with you. We've talked about our ROI and why that's important and how, as an Admin, we can bring back the value to the team. We've talked about some great lead-gen systems too. Like what you can do to protect the Agent's time and hold them accountable. Next is the importance of the lead-gen for you. We've talked about the system; now let's talk about the importance.

One of the things I want to leave you with is a small piece of homework for this chapter. I was hoping you could develop a plan on how you, as an individual, can promote your team or your Agent, depending on your team's size in terms of social media, email blasts, etc. You can create your database within the team and solely focus on the people that you add to the database in a way that looks like you're talking to them.

You want to create increased brand awareness, so brand yourself on social media. We will do a whole chapter on marketing, so I'm not going to go deep into this one little tool that I found to be successful. I learned this in one of the training classes I attended years ago. This one stuck with me, and it was one of the first things I implemented for myself when I joined our team.

I got comfortable with understanding the lead-gen system and having a database of my own. I created a list of twenty people that I knew I could add to the database, such as, family, friends, people I found on Facebook and in my friend's contact lists. Every day, I started putting twenty people into the database. I create that list of twenty people and then I create another list of twenty, or more, people. These are going be the people in your community; your doctors, your lawyers, people who are at your dentist office, your nail salon people, your hairdresser, your teachers, your principals, your hockey families, your hockey coaches . . . Think outside the box.

Once your lists are created, start to create your email blast. Now, before you add people to the database, you need to make sure that you have their permission. That's one thing that I stand firm on. Our rules are a little bit different than those of an Agent. It's a simple conversation with your dentist, before or after your appointment. You could say, "I don't know if you know this, but I've entered the world of Real Estate and I work for such and such team. I'd love to add you to our database." What you'll get is just the value of any upcoming listings we have, Open Houses or any general events that we throw, or host, within the community. It's just an added value to you. I would love if you'd be part of it."

Most times, people will say yes because nobody wants to say no, and the worst thing that can happen is they will unsubscribe. We give them the power to unsubscribe if they want to. I want you to understand the importance of our Return on Investment and its efforts. Not a lot of Administrators think to go that way. They don't think that they can add their people to the database until they're ready to buy or sell. The truth is, you're not talking to your family and friends all the time. If you can, set them up on your email and only send them certain things. What an amazing reach for your team. Your team will be at top-of-mind for your friends and family.

I've even taken it as far as posting on social media asking things like, "Who wants to be set up to our team's email blast? Here's the value you will get . . ." Then, I would list all the emails that we send out. Now, mind you, not everybody jumped in, but you'd be surprised at how many people agree to be set up mainly because they want to support you. Remember, while you're supporting somebody else, someone's going to support you.

I was able to build a database by simply asking my social media contacts for permission. It's a great value add, and I would love to see you guys start writing down your list of twenty contacts and creating a template, or an ad, or a campaign for them. We'll get into that stuff in the database chapter, for sure. I would love to hear your success stories around this, so please feel free to reach out to me and share them.

Steps to Get You Started

- Time-block your lead-gen hours
- Goal plan—how many contacts a day
- How are you going to lead-gen
- Share all this info with your Admin

Create a long-term system around lead-gen, so this can be built out if you decide to grow a team. Add all new contacts to the CRM immediately, with a follow-up reminder . . . more details to come. Know that at the moment, no matter how hard this is for you, do not stop these actions. I never want to bring down a mood, but when you are not lead-generating and building a pipeline, you've stopped creating opportunities for your Admin and, more importantly, your future.

These tools work, and I am proof. I write this to share success and save you all from making the mistakes our team did. These systems will have you at a high level in no time. It's within you! You have yourself, your family, and your Admin to think about. It's a lot. I will also hold your Admin to the same high accountability as I do you! I will show them it's possible to build a lead-gen funnel as an Admin, as well as generate additional units outside the forty you goal planned for in the second chapter. Crazy, right? But so effective!

Key Takeaways from This Chapter

Okay, we are going to close up chapter four. I hope I haven't given you too much to think about and put too much pressure on you about the importance of lead-gen, but it is detrimental to your business if you do not have a good lead-gen system in place. Especially if you're looking to grow because it'll encourage other Agents; it'll look appealing for recruiting, etc. So have a good plan in place that has good systems around it, as well. Admins, make sure you're documenting your lead-gen system.

I want to share a quick story with you about our lead-gen experience with our team, that's been the basis of this chapter, the basic foundation that we have for our lead-gen system. We're a larger team at the point where we have Agents who are lead-generating. Their commitment to the team is to lead-gen two hours a day, Monday to Friday. It was kind of the reason why I've put some of these things in this chapter because these are examples from our team and the success that we have from them. So please bear with me with this story. I hope you enjoy it because it has been a really big factor in our success.

When I started with our team, it was just me and one other person, our team leader. The man just picks up the phone and calls, no fear. Not only did he go right in and ask for the business; most times, he asked for referrals. He wasn't afraid. It wasn't abrasive. He has a very amazing approach to these things and it comes from script practicing. He never practices on his clients. He just knows that he wants to grow a business. He loves listing properties. He loves helping families and he can't do that if he doesn't lead-gen. People saw how hard he worked and saw that from 9:00 a.m. to 11:00 a.m., every day, he had a noise-cancelling headset on so he can tune out his surroundings and focus on the call. His CRM was open; he did use his cell phone. This was at a point where he used his cell phone. I never let anyone distract him.

We were in a space where it was just the two of us, and, it was the size of a closet. There was no other space for me to go to anywhere else so, I just listened to the lead-gen and we just happen to be in an office where there were other Agents around, too. It was a big office space and we just had this little nook part of it. He was able to motivate other teams to lead-gen. He just created this energy in the office. We finally bought our own space to build our team. It was part of the commitment. Every Agent comes in and they lead-gen from 9:00 a.m. to 11:00 a.m., Monday to Friday.

Now, from Monday to Wednesday, from 9:00 a.m. to 11:00 a.m. was lead-gen and cold-calling time and we used a system called Mojo Triple Line Dialer. We're just continuously calling over and over again, different numbers. We target certain areas that we consider our farming area. We got hung up on several times, told really bad things. Often people told us to "F" off. There was a lot of negativity around it and I think that's why we're uncomfortable doing it. But the reality of it is if you push through those uncomfortable calls, and learn to handle objections, you'll grow a thick skin. Not everyone we call understands what we're doing, and that's fine. Then you find that gold, that one person who answers your call and says, "You know, I've been thinking about having a realtor come in. Thanks for calling." You have to grind through.

Real Estate isn't sexy, but it can be fun, and you can make a lot of money doing it. You have to put the work in, and I find lead-gen is the dirty part of the Agents' jobs; the ones where we watch you guys grind it out. We watch the upsets, not reaching your goals, not booking appointments, but you've just got to keep going. We're your biggest fans. We're watching this happen and we see the struggles. We may not be right there getting those people who hang upon you, but we feel it because we see it on you. Keep pushing. That's exactly what our team did.

Thursday to Friday, our team door-knocks, so they replace cold-calling with door-knocking. We call it a race and replace whatever you're erasing from your lead-gen calendar. What are you replacing it with? There's going to be door-knocking. We would have notes printed: Open House this Weekend, Just Sold in your Neighborhood, or Looking for a Market Report . . . All the fun stuff. We actually door-knocked and spoke to people. We got the contact information. One of the most amazing things is when you're able to talk about it and look at the stats. We would sit down every October of our year in business, planning events and going through our lead source funnel. Where did the majority of our business come from? Then it would go as far as asking ourselves, "What type of lead-gen was successful?"

As our team grew, things changed. There were things, such as, do not call lists and the Mojo Triple Line Dialer that became more of a chore than a money-making activity, which wasn't effective. Our team noticed, in our second year of business planning, that Mojo cold-calling was at the bottom of our lead-gen sources. We decided to take a break, however, we replaced it with additional door-knocking, now going to new farm areas and introducing the team. We replaced the Mojo with this form of lead-gen. We've also taken it and replaced it with social media marketing, or some social media lead-gen, where we follow up with our friends on Facebook and Instagram.

As long as you have a plan and stick with it to see it through, the proof is in the numbers. The proof is always in the numbers. Have a set lead-gen system with Admins documenting every step, we have templates in place for door-knocking and we have farm accounts set up in Mojo.

Be very purposeful with everything that you do. Our team built a strong lead-gen system for two years. We reached a point where we had to change it up because we needed something new. People have heard from us, we've called these areas several times, so we had to change it up. Then COVID-19 hit, and we started going back to lead-gen and cold-calling people. It was a huge game-changer for us. We changed the value of our calls. We didn't call people to say, "Hey, times are tough. Are you looking to sell?" That is the worst thing we could do to anybody at that time. We called and checked in on people. Some people got upset and others appreciated our call. We started connecting with clients and providing value in any way we could during the pandemic. We mentioned, "We are all struggling right now and we have ways that we can we help you. We have access to resources. We have a really big vendor list of people. If you need anything at all, please don't hesitate to ask us for help. That's all we're here for right now." The result is we've built a pipeline, and, more importantly, we just built a huge trust within our community and the people in the areas we called have the value in our calls. All the best to you and go get them.

CHAPTER 5

COMMUNICATION

Most Important Tool in Partnership

Why a whole chapter on communication? I know it isn't very appealing, but it is essential, and without proper communication there will be no foundation. Communication builds trust, ownership, and growth for both Admin and Agent. Communication then moves toward your clients and shows up in all you do. This chapter is going to focus on communication tools to help you and your Empire Builder build. It is important that once you hire your Admin, the foundation is set for communication tools between yourselves and your clients. This book is about laying the foundation for growth.

You might ask how you can make more money from reading a book. I am about to communicate all those answers. Building a business takes energy, systems, models, passion, and you need to lay a foundation for a sustainable business. This book is showing you how to do that by taking small steps to run a high-level business. I know this works because my team is living proof of that. The following are the best communication practices for you and your Admin and, eventually, the team's growth. Commitment to these best practices is also required. Before I tell you about all the best communication methods, please commit right now to at least picking one method and start with it.

Weekly one-on-one meetings with your Admin are important. Preferably on a Monday so you can cover the week and everything that is needed. Create a plan or an outline, so nothing is missed in this meeting, and don't go over thirty minutes unless you are working on some big projects.

Side Tip: When discussing big projects in a meeting, have a blank paper for the projects. Label it with a title to prevent it from getting lost in the general plan.

Morning Huddle: As you grow, have meetings every morning, via phone, or in person. Take five minutes to get the day started. A lot of successful people like to share motivation before they start the day. It could even be a simple video for a quick jumpstart motivation of the day. As you grow, so does communication.

In one of my chapters, I mentioned the end of day email and four important questions your Admin should answer at the end of the day. This frees you from worries about what was done, what needs to get done, etc.

Team Meeting: Again, it could be every Monday to go over numbers, Open Houses, new listings, etc. Focus on the numbers and where you need to be, where you are at, and so on. If you are growing a Real Estate team, this will be a huge piece of communication for you as a leader and your entire team. Have a whiteboard, success planners, or excel sheet with all your numbers in front of you, so you know your goals and visions. The next piece will focus on the importance of culture and communication. Why did I add the two together? Because culture flows from our words and communication with others.

The Importance of Culture/Communication

We have all heard the phrase "lead by example," and as a leader, you are constantly under a microscope with your Admin, your community, etc. We all want someone we can look up to and strive to be like; your Admin is that person, as well. If they said yes to working with you, it isn't the fact they needed a job, at all. You triggered something in them that made them want to work *with you*!

When I met my team leader years ago, the energy and the vision he had was so powerful. I couldn't picture myself being around anyone else. This person's vision was so big that I could have a big vision for me within it. He leads by example, every single day in his words and actions.

Culture is another form of communication. How will you motivate one another? Seriously, take a minute and think about how the two of you will lift each other when you are weak?

How will you move forward in hard times? What culture do you need to practice to be those versions of yourselves? Empire Builders, I am here to tell you those days will be there. You will need to wake up and inspire your Agent to keep going. Your positivity and your words of encouragement are needed. That's what we do! We lead with a servant's heart, and we lead our leaders through tough times just as they do for us. Culture isn't how you want to be perceived; it's how you want to be. It attracts talent, opportunity, and clients to work with you. You show your culture in everything you do.

Culture/Communication

Culture is symbolic communication. I said it before, at the beginning of this chapter, and I'm going to say it again. How do you motivate one another? Take a moment and think about how the two of you will lift each other when you are weak, how you will move forward in hard times. We need culture to be those best versions of ourselves.

There will be days where your agents lack focus and structure. It's not because of a lack of wanting you there. It's a communication breakdown. The minute there's a communication breakdown, culture is typically the first thing to go out the window. We start getting upset. We start assuming things. Culture is the symbolic communication. It's in our words and our actions. It's what we do with one another and how we treat one another.

You're going to have days where you need to wake up and inspire your Agent to keep going, even when you're not sure you can keep going yourself. Your positivity and your words of encouragement are needed. That's what we do. We lead with a servant's heart and we lead our leadership through tough times. Never underestimate the power of an Administrator; we persevere. That's what we do. When our Agents are down, we lift them up. Culture isn't how you want to be perceived; it's who you are. It goes back to those quotes I shared earlier. It's a way of life, in your behaviours, your beliefs, your values.

You then take all that, and you express it through communication. It attracts talent, opportunities, and clients who want to work with you. You show your client's culture in everything you do, whether it's negative or positive. The choice is yours. How often do you lose a listing? When you lose a listing, do you blame it on others? Do you blame it on the clients? Do you blame it on your Admin? It could be all of the above. Imagine taking that anger and reflecting it into a learning opportunity and taking full responsibility for that last listing paperwork that was done incorrectly for a client you weren't connecting with. It all boils down to you and complete ownership. That's a hard pill to swallow for some, and as a leader, you own that. You own it all. It takes courage to own up to mistakes, whether they're yours or not and that's the kind of leader Admins look to when you come back, and you didn't get the listing appointment.

To be honest, I don't like to use that as an example (not getting the listing), but it happens. We want to also be open to hearing the feedback as to why we didn't get the listing and what we could have done better. We want to learn from that because your loss is our loss. We celebrate together, and we learn together. Taking opportunity from our losses and turning them into learning lessons is important no matter how hard. And that's building the culture.

You want to get inside your Admins' head and figure out what makes us work harder. It isn't money. I mean, that's nice and rewarding, but it isn't the money. It's watching you in action, confidently learning to grow and doing so with such positivity. It's the environment you create, the energy, and the vibes you build that lead and inspire us to grow a business with you. One word: *karma*. What you put out into the universe comes back to you. If you create a negative environment and bring your Admin down every day, you won't have an Empire Builder; you'll have an empty desk and possibly no business coming in, in a few months, because there's no one to help you.

Communication and culture are up there as a strong force in our business. As a negotiator and lead-generator, the gift of communication is your most valuable tool in sales and your Admin can match that energy when you lead by example. Negative communication and culture lead to abandoned roles and, more importantly, abandoned clients.

We're talking about our relationship and what we can do for one another when, in reality, it's the client who is first and foremost in this entire transaction. Breakdown in communication leads to big mistakes and a sour reputation when business is also built on repeats and referrals. We always tell our clients the truth, no matter how hard it can be. It's the most important tool you have. Most clients will respect honesty. Being honest might not always feel good for both parties, but they respect it and it's the right thing to do.

We're going to jump into who benefits from the communication. Why do I benefit from great communication? I want you to ask yourself that. Who benefits from communication? Your client does, your Admin does, your business does, and that all leads back to you. This entire chapter is on communication and the tools to be a good communicator. Towards the end of the chapter, I will give you three techniques for great communication and tracking communication. Make sure you have a pen and paper handy. You don't need to do all of them. Pick one that works best for you and do it well. Do it at a high-level right from the start.

So, first things first, can you/will you commit to building culture within? How do you start building an amazing MVV? Do you want to run a business? Do you want to create legacies for your kids, family? Do you want to bring value in your community? If you said "yes," then please sit down! Before you grow into a Real Estate team/business, build an MVV, and share that everywhere you can. Let your clients and community know you are here for the long run, and here is what you offer.

I'm going to add something here, just so I don't forget. It goes back to understanding what your culture is. Some people might not know what culture is for them and feel overwhelmed, and they don't know what they want their Admin to focus on. They don't know how to communicate properly. Here's the thing, and don't panic, everyone struggles with this. There is no easy way. You'll find your groove, and then you may lose it, but you'll find your groove again. As I said, I'm going to share some systems with you at the end, but here's how we can get laser focused, which was a very important part for our team while moving forward. It is the heart of our team. Are you wondering what an MVV is? We created what is called Missions, Visions, and Values (MVV). We strictly only hire to culture when we go through the process. I mentioned it in the interview part of this book on hiring your ideal teammate. As we grew as a team, one of the things we put in place was an ideal teammate chart for any future hires, both Admin and Agent.

We asked ourselves who do we want to work with and what does that person look like. We only hire to culture and here's the reason for that; you can be a top salesperson crushing listing appointments and bringing buyers in, the whole bit, but if you don't have the culture, it means nothing to us. We're not building a business on the money. We're building it on our clients and our future. Hiring someone just because they're a top salesperson but don't have the team's communication skills, is like a drop of red dye in your water bucket. Slowly, it seeps in and the water turns red over time, not right away. So, it's very important when you're continuing to build a team, or grow, you always come back to what is culture.

One of the best ways to figure out what culture is in your MVV is taking the opportunity to put something together so you can share with your clients. It can be part of your listing appointment. You can brand it and put it on your wall. Knowing your mission, what the vision is for your team, and the values you hold, shows that you're running a high-level business and, clients love it.

We decided as a team we needed a Mission Statement, one that whenever confronted with issues we always come back to that statement. After forty-eight hours, multiple emails and a lot of team meetings around it, our team finally figured out what our mission was. Once we established our Mission Statement, we immediately branded it and shared it with our clients Our Mission Statement is also everything we think of and everything we do. Our Mission Statement is, "Building trust with our clients so our clients can build better lives." Every time we have something that gets us off track, we always take a minute and say, "Is this building trust with our clients?" Then, whatever that answer is, we take our steps from there. So, take some time. This isn't going to take a minute. This will not take an hour. This might take weeks for you to consider. But once you brand your MVV, you can share that during your listing presentations, etc., because it solidifies you. I think it warms your heart. You're building a big picture, here, and you're sharing it with others.

One of the important things to get from this book is writing your Mission, Visions, and Values. If you do, please find me on social media and tag me in it. Share it with me because I love it when people take the time to create that.

Who benefits from communication? I think this answer is pretty obvious, but if your answer is you, I would like you to ask yourself that again. Your client benefits from communication, your Admin benefits, your business benefits, and that all leads back to you. Seriously, this is a whole chapter on communication and tools to be a good communicator. How many of you attempted script practicing? Role-playing? If you haven't, I suggest you find a great scripting partner. Someone better at getting clients than you and work with them. It doesn't need to be a long venture. Fifteen minutes a day is beneficial. It's a known fact that you should never practice on your clients, and many of us do.

Methods of Communication

We're going to switch gears here for a minute to talk about the types of communication. Toward the end of the chapter, I'm going to break down some great forms of communication for you. One of the things I want you to consider before you finish this book and kind of have action plan in place is: do your script practicing and role-playing. I don't mean the fun kind of role-playing outside of work. I mean role-playing your listing presentations. Your sit-down meeting, your new buyer presentations. The general statement I hear all the time is that we should never practice on our clients, and the majority of us do. A lot of us have probably never heard that statement, and that's okay. But I'm telling you now; we should not be practicing on our clients. So how do we not practice on our clients? Find a good script partner. Look for someone at your brokerage, on your team, outside of your team, from another brokerage event, someone who looks to be doing a great job at booking appointments with clients, maybe better than you.

Script practicing and role-playing should take no more than fifteen minutes per person. Fifteen minutes a day is very beneficial. A lot of top teams in our industry live and breathe this practice every day. If you do not do script practicing, I suggest finding somebody that can help you with this. Leverage your Admin to help look for others and ask if anyone's willing to script practice and role-play with you.

Admins, as you're reading this, this is where your Agent needs support. An Admin should also be able to communicate if not as good as you, better. Because when your client calls and they can't reach you, your Admin steps in to take your call. It will be as though there is no difference, and they are getting the exact type of client service they would get if you had answered the phone.

We're going to reach a point, Admins, where clients don't even want to talk to the Agents. They want to talk to you, solely, and the leverage that you give your client or your Agent at that moment is priceless. When a client calls and says, "Hi (Admin), I was just calling to talk to you because I know that I will get the answer a little bit faster than if I was talking to (Agent)." I love those calls.

Side Note: If this does happen, and I am speaking from experience, you might not have the answers, right away, for a client when they do call. So, here is what you are going to do; we call this "under-promising and over-delivering," and it will always win the day. You can say, "You know what, 'so and so' isn't in the office today but I am happy to help with your questions. Give me until the end of the day to get an answer for you and I'll call you back." You hang up the phone. You search high and low for that answer. You call that client back before the end of the day, preferably within the next couple of hours, and that is how you build a client experience. Now, they're probably thinking, "Oh, I didn't anticipate hearing back to you from you until the end of the day." So, you're giving them a great experience. We're going to do a chapter on client services and client experiences, as well. That's going to be a chapter strictly for your Administrators.

The following are a few great tools to start communication, how we can communicate on the outside and communicate with one another. As I said, you don't need to do all of these at once. You can pick one that works well and go with it. Before we finish, I also want to talk about the power of positivity and the power of positive thinking. It's imperative, as a leader, that you hold this skill when times get tough and you start to get down. Remember, people are watching you, and those people are your Admins, your team, all the people that look up to you. You're going to have people you've inspired along the way because people will want to know how you're doing it.

If you can double your deals because of an Administrator, people will want to know what your secret formula is to succeed. I'm not going to lie. I always say the secret weapon is your Administrator. So, when I say the power of positive thinking, it's not letting the negative thoughts overcome you.

If you're somebody who really struggles around negativity and always kind of looks to the bad side of things, then seek some methods around positive thinking and focus on shifting the way you look at things. When you shift the way you look at things, it opens up the opportunity to see things differently. Your Empire Builder should be able to communicate just as well, if not better than you, so that when your client calls them because they can't get a hold of you, your Admin will be able to speak on your behalf.

An Empire Builder will reach a point where the client will always call them first, before you, and don't take it personally.

It's just that they will have the answers and they will be able to walk the client through the process, just as well as you could at one time. That's what you want! You want someone who will care for your clients more than you do. Culture and communication will get you there. We will get into some great tools for communication, which is outside the how to communicate with one another realm.

Have a great CRM/database where you store *all* your communication with clients and with each other. You can document all client info and notes you take during your call and notify your Admin team that you just spoke with a client, what the outcome was, and vice versa. There will be a whole chapter dedicated to the database so we will touch on this more.

Group texting system with you and your Admin. Our team uses WhatsApp for all communication outside of client notes, outside normal business hours, and we use this tool to celebrate wins and success stories.

Use journals to record your thoughts and anything you need to remind your team, or yourself, of. Close out your day with writing down ideas, marketing suggestions, who you need to reach out to tomorrow, what you need your Admin to do, etc. Utilize this and send it to your Admin to make sure they have their to-do list ready for them in the morning. This is a huge asset to communication and saves so much time and energy in the process.

We just completed a whole chapter on communication and thank you for seeing the value in this. I promise you that with strong communication and focus on culture, you will have an incredible foundation, again, for your business. Now Agents, your goal is to find a script partner and one method of communication that you can implement for you and your Admin—your Empire Builder. Empire Builders, your goal is to hold your Agents accountable to finding a script partner and implementing communication tools for you both.

CHAPTER 6

DATABASE

The Gold is in the Database

I hope you guys are still following me and enjoying what you are reading because you are going to love this chapter. This chapter is going to talk to you about the importance of a strong database. This is something that we typically talk about at the beginning of your business, or beginning of training or coaching, because it is one of the most essential tools for your business. When we first get started, many of us use an Excel spreadsheet for our contacts or, you know, some even keep contacts in their cell phones. There is nothing wrong with that method. It is just not scalable, nor is it reliable enough to grow your business. That is why we are here, the different types of databases and how you can leverage an Administrator to utilize this as a key component to communication, building relationships, and the overall success of your client's information.

One of the things we should talk about, upfront, is making sure you have permission when you add someone to the database, especially with all the rules and regulations around privacy. So, it is really important that the first thing you do is seek approval to invite that person into your database. Once they have agreed to everything, you can start hitting them with the emails, the phone calls and whatever it is your database does for you. One tip I can give you right now is to never add anyone to the database currently working with a realtor, or if they are in contract and closing on a transaction. It is just a great way to start fresh and to keep the database clean.

To start, what is a database? You can call it a database. Some people will call it a data bank. Some people call it a CRM. You will hear lots of terms for databases. I am going to use the word database throughout this chapter, as just one term for all of us to understand. Truth is, we call it a database because that is where you store your data, your client information, phone numbers, email addresses, anything related to your client and their information.

As you grow—whether it is just you, or an Admin, or you decide to grow a team—this is where all your communication is entered. This is where all your marketing plans go. This is where all your client information ends up. There is so much value in this database and we are going to talk about the value within it towards the end of this chapter.

So, how do you set up a strong database? We have talked about communication and we have talked about hiring. Now it is time to set up your database for success, if you have not already. I want you to stop using an Excel spreadsheet. But before you stop using that sheet, I want you to implement a strong CRM. Do not leave your contacts on your phone, invest in a database. There are a lot of them on the market to choose from. Do your research. Here is where you would leverage your Admin to help, as well.

How do you know what database is right for you? Whatever database you choose to work with today, stick with it. Determine how it can work for you before giving up and moving back to the way things were, whether it is that Excel spreadsheet or your contacts in your phone. You cannot effectively work with your Administrator, in terms of communication around a client, with your phone contacts. It is just not a scalable system to have. Give your database to your Admin once you found the right CRM and let them build it out to help build your business.

It is very simple; your Admin will have all the access and be able to communicate with your clients when you can't. Based on the information you provided in the database. All you need to do is input the client's information and let your Admin handle everything else. They will take it over from there. They can create campaigns, marketing strategies, email blasts, and follow-ups all from the CRM.

When you are deciding what CRM you would like to use, think of one that's scalable. If you are looking to build a team, do not buy a CRM, or invest in a CRM, for the moment. Invest in a CRM that is scalable to add more people to your team as you grow. Your Administrator will help to build your business and build a strong follow-up system around it. In this chapter, I am going to list three of my top CRM tips to ensure success within the database for you and your Admin. Now just understand the importance of how to build a strong foundation around it. It is one of the most essential tools you will ever use.

There is a popular phrase that many Agents use, especially in my brokerage, and it's "the gold is in the database." I never fully understood that until working in this industry. I am going to walk you through systems and tools that we use in our team. I can list types of CRMs for you to use, as well, but the reality of it is that it must fit with what you need. It must be something that you can build out, like I mentioned earlier, something that you can take from day one and build on it as your team grows, and as your business grows.

Make sure the CRM you choose is not one that fits you right now. I cannot express that enough. Make sure it is the one that is going to fit your needs years from now. You want to ask yourself, when doing your research, what do you want from your database? Can it send large emails? Can it hold enough contacts to send those emails? What about websites, landing pages, SEO? There are so many top-of-the-line CRMs out there right now that have so many amazing features and can bring so much value. You have to do the research to find out what fits best for you.

How powerful of a CRM do you need? Where do you see your business in a year? This is important when you start looking for your CRM. You will know what you're looking for when you jump online to start researching your options and you have the ability to watch YouTube videos. See how others interact with those CRMs and databases to understand if it's something that you can fully function for yourself and your Administrator. Find out what they're all capable of doing. Look at the products within your database, or CRM. If you're not very tech savvy, that's okay. I'm not the best with technology either, when it comes to this stuff. I just had a strong vision on what our team needed so that's what I looked for in our database/CRM.

Utilize your Empire Builder. I've said that before. When researching CRMs, have your Admin write down all of the key things you're looking for in a database. These are the things that you want to make sure your potential database/CRM can do. When you're asking your Admin to help you research and bring options to you, don't spend too much time on it yourself and don't overthink it. Create a timeline. Give your Admin some options for databases and/or CRMs that you want to look into. In a week or so, have your Admin report back on what they've established to be the best CRM to move forward with. Make sure a goal is in place during this research, so your Admin knows that this is something you're serious about. Allow your Admin to give insight on their research because the reality is 50 percent of the usage in the database is going to be made by your Administrator—your Empire Builder. They're going to create your marketing plans and all of the other stuff that goes into your day-to-day operations.

We are also going to touch a little bit about how to divide up your database and maximize your follow-ups, using an *ABC* system that many teams utilize (ourselves included). So right now, let's just say for the sake of this chapter, you have your database, you've chosen your CRM, you've made the decision, and you've invested so wisely. So, what's next? You're going to want to take all the contacts that are in that phone, and in your Excel spreadsheet, and transfer them into your database. This will be the first place to start, and you are going to want to transfer them all in. If you are familiar with a CSV file, you can utilize that for transferring your contacts. Most of the CRM companies will come with a support staff, or resource library, that will help you get your contacts into your database, so use that. Don't try to do this all on your own. You don't have the time. Leverage your Admin again, and the support that comes with the CRM from the companies.

You want to have a clean database from the start. That's really important and that's my golden rule. Many people go in and just put in the basic minimum information and then a year from now, as your team grows and you've expanded your client database, you have a mess. You don't have postal codes, you don't have email addresses, you have inaccurate or not up-to-date information around your clients, your clients may have moved. It's an absolute mess. Do not let this happen. If you read this chapter all the way to the end and you can implement these, then you're setting yourself up for success.

Right now, I'm showing you how to start strong so you don't have to go back and clean up as often as a lot of Agents do. I'm giving you golden nuggets. Here's the #1 tip to database success; all client information that goes into the database needs to be correct, from the beginning. That includes email addresses, postal codes, phone numbers and home addresses. Start off on the right foot. If there is anything you can take away from this chapter it's that you need to start with all the correct information in the database so you don't have to go back months later and make corrections. Start strong . . . I can't emphasize this enough.

This chapter is a formula for success in itself. All the client information that you have, and your ability to get it into the database, generates your revenue, moving forward. Once you are set up and your contacts are uploaded to the database, you can begin looking at all the avenues of marketing plans and follow-up systems—whether it be your phone calls, text messages, email blasts, or social media. Make sure the information is correct when it goes into the database because it will make the process for everything we just mentioned that much more streamlined. There should be no reason why your Agents should not have a 100 percent clean database from this moment on if they are utilizing you to go back and ensure that all the information is there. If you ever want to send a new greeting card, a Christmas card, or even a Happy Birthday card, you have the address in there already and it makes life so much easier for you.

This step can take years for Agents to do correctly and I'm hoping you can sense the passion in my voice around this. It will save you so much time and energy doing it right, the first time. Some of you might already have a CRM in place. From this moment forward I want you to commit to putting all the information needed around your client into the database correctly. This goes back to our chapter on communication; the importance of communication and being authentic with your client. If you can't communicate, have your Admin step in for you by reading the notes in the database and being able to finish the conversation you've had with your client. It's a great client experience.

Let's say it together, "The #1 tip is that all the correct information goes into the database on day one." Make sure your database has reminders. This is another key to success. This is a tool that most people don't actually think about often, and it has taken us years to get there ourselves. This is a tool that we now preach about consistently. Once you add a contact into the database, your next step is to set up the reminder, immediately. A reminder, for those of you who are new to this, let's you know when to take the next step with your client. This is a key component that you can set up for yourself. It will lead you into success for your follow-up schedules. Setting a reminder is as simple as going in after you've added all the information and planning the next step. When do you want to speak to your client next? Plan the next touch point and set your reminder immediately, before you close down the contact.

A perfect example of typical reminders is: Is it one week out or a three-month follow-up? Once you have established that you can create a great system around reminders. A good CRM, when you log into it, will have a dashboard that will show you a list of your follow-up calls for the day. You should be able to click on that client and immediately be logged into a phone call, and/or email. In this situation, if you're setting up a meeting, add your Admin to the calendar, as well, so that they can help support you and set the meeting up for you. They will take care of all the stuff behind the scenes to get you set up for your meeting. With every client, you start your follow-up system the minute they have been imported into the database. That way when you log into your CRM, you'll know what follow-ups you have for the day. You know how much time it will take to make those follow-up calls, and more importantly, the value of connecting with a client through the follow-up. The expectations set from the initial point of contact, creates rapport and builds trust. Step one is adding accurate information into the database. Step two is the reminder set for the next time you're going to communicate with your client. Here's where you're going to leverage your Admin.

Here is my third tip for success. This is where your Admin is going to shine behind the scenes and create 8x8 campaigns for you. I'm not going to get into those details right now, because that we will do in a whole other chapter about marketing, where I will give you examples of a simple 8x8 campaign. This is where your Admin will set you up for success with campaign marketing for email blasts, social media, community events and mailouts. That right there is the third step to a successful database. If you're not doing that right now, please make that one of the first things you do. If you're feeling overwhelmed and unsure if you can do this, go back through this with your Administrators.

What happens when we don't have a successfully clean database from the very beginning? This is where you're going to slow down and delegate a cleanup system. It could be once a quarter, or once a month, depending on the size of your database. It also needs to be updated, which means going inside and ensuring the contact information for your clients is still accurate and up-to-date. Nobody really wants to do this type of job. It's a heavy data entry task. I understand we have a lot of important things to do; that is why I am constantly reminding you to keep things clean from the beginning because none of those above marketing techniques will matter without the correct client information.

The database is the main spot of the hub, the heart of all client communication. Whatever conversations you have with the client, you must immediately put the notes into the database. That way your Agent can pick up where you left off, or vice versa. Always think of step one, two and three and I promise you, you will have the best routine and best formula for a successful database.

We're about to jump into the next part here, quickly. I'm going to try to make it as simple as possible for all of you to understand the next key component of the database setup, because this is where things get a little bit tricky. First of all, I want to talk about the ABCs of the database, and what they are. Often, especially if you're in a relationship-based business, the first thing you want to do is start building your database and this, for me, is a strategy that has worked for our team.

The value in the ABC system is labelling your database. In the first part of this chapter, we talked about reminders, correct information and marketing campaigns. The next step here is how important labelling your database is. ABC has always been the method that we've used in our team and it works well. In your database, determine what level your clients are at. *A* clients are typically those zero to three months out of purchase or currently in transaction and looking, and you're actively showing them houses or their house is on the market with you. *B* clients are four to six months out and *C* clients are seven to twelve months out.

I'm not sure if a lot of you are familiar with the phrase, "the pond," in a database. Our team established a pond section where we put contacts that we've never connected with. Invalid phone number, but correct email addresses with no response. We don't want to lose them, but we know that they're not as active as our As, Bs and Cs. You're probably asking why this is important to do. Well, it boils down to very effective database control for you. You will have more clarity on how you're going to turn contacts into As.

I will create a chart below for you to review and go into more detail on what an A looks like, what a B looks like and how often you're communicating with all of them. If you know that people in your database are looking to transact in twelve months or so, you're still going to make sure they have a follow-up system, and that they're hooked up to all of your marketing strategies. I want you to go through your database with your Admin and purposely categorize your clients. What an amazing start to a great follow-up schedule. Be very purposeful with your time and knowing what's in your database. It is essential, when having a powerful database, that your database can single-handedly have complete control over your business. Between the database and your numbers, these are two systems that need your constant attention.

Something that is also important and I think you've heard this before, is now that you have a database, you've got to feed it. What does that system look like? How many people are you going to be adding to your database and setting you up for success? I intend to add twenty contacts a day, as an example, or I intend to add one hundred contacts a week. Know what your goal is to feed your database and whatever your choice is; it comes back to your goal planning.

I've given you the steps to set up your database. I've given you a breakdown of the As, Bs and Cs. Now, one of the other things I'm going to talk to you about, before we jump into the end of this chapter, is labelling your database. The reason why I'm going to talk about it now is that it's going to set you up for additional success. As we move through this chapter, you'll understand a strong 8x8 campaign, and how labelling is extremely important. Make sure you look for the options to categorize and label your database. When researching, look for CRMs that give the option to label or categorize your database. I will share a general list of labels you can use for your database to get started:

- Past Clients
- Realtors
- Downsize
- First Time Homebuyers
- Retirement

- Sphere
- VIP
- Renewal

Every contact in the database needs a label, and that is essential for future growth. When you get to the part where you're growing, and you have to transition somebody from first time homebuyer to now a repeat client, you will need to be laser focused on your database. Not only are you growing your database, you've got people in the right categories and you know how to communicate with each and every one of them.

Now let's talk about communicating with them. Let's say you have ten realtors in your database, all from different brokerages or all from the same brokerage—it doesn't matter. You want to send out an email blast for a career night or for an agent only Open House. Instead of having to send an email blast to your entire database in hopes that one realtor sees it and plucks it out of thin air, you're only going to focus on sending the email to the realtors labelled in your database. That's it! If you don't already have lead sources in there, or labels on your clients, have your Admin go through it and do it for you.

One of the other reasons labelling is good for your database is, let's say you are holding a first-time homebuyer's seminar and you have so many spaces allotted for your event and you want to send an email blast out to all your first-time homebuyers in the database. You can do so with ease because you have already labelled the people who are first time homebuyers. Now you're probably thinking, "Why not send it out to everybody?" Somebody might know someone who is a first-time homebuyer. At times, we often go that route, but this is when you want to be laser focused, protect your time, and be very purposeful with your events that you create through your database. This is where labelling your database comes in handy. We also like to have what we call a VIP system. We want people to feel that we are very focused on them, and very appreciative and grateful for the business that they have given us in return. Typically, our VIP events are an invite only situation.

Now, we're going to jump right into this next part and talk about the value within your database. Your Admin should be just as strong with this skill, around the database, as you are. In fact, I want them to be one step better than you. Knowing the value of your database is huge. Knowing the value of each client in your database is an incredible power to have.

I'm going to give you an example of value within the database, and I'm going to be honest because it's very hard for me to share these types of stories. I'm a very relationship-based person and I never look at our clients as commission. I don't see the value in a business with that kind of mindset. I was at a training event, a few years ago, and they spoke about the value within the database. In that moment, it stopped me in my tracks and made me think, "Do I know the value in our database?" It doesn't take away from the fact that I love our clients, but I had to take a moment and think about what the value in the database means and how important it is to understand the value in each person I add.

One of the reasons I feel so strongly about understanding the value of a database is based off the following story.

I'm about to share with you an experience our team had a few years ago. We have a client in our database, right now, whom of which we did a deal with. In my world, it was Saturday morning and I was at a hockey tournament. This client called me and said, "My husband and I have found our dream home. You don't know me, but my husband and I get a lot of your marketing material and all of Chris's (my Agent) phone calls. You're not our biggest fans. My husband isn't your biggest fan." I immediately thought, "Oh, no, why is she calling me then?" So, when I asked her, I said, "Okay, I'm so sorry. Is there anything I can do for you?" Her response was, "Yes, could you please get me in to look at this new home. With of all your marketing, your calls and your follow-up calls, you were the first people I thought to reach out to. Your magnet hangs on my fridge, you've door-knocked my house, and you seem to work really hard. So, if we like this house, we will be wanting to list our own." We ended up helping her to not only purchase her dream home but sell her current home. We did an amazing job of helping this family sell and purchase their dream home. She is a perfect example of giving the ultimate client experience. We do this for every single client we work with. She was wonderful from the very beginning; easy to work with. She got along with our entire team. Her and her family became part of our team throughout the entire transaction.

For the sake of giving this client a name, I'm going call her Patty. Patty was the perfect example of when you spend time with your clients, getting to know their needs and their wants and understanding what's important to them, it can create the ultimate client experience. We left her family feeling heard, helped, and, more importantly, living in their dream home. Patty has become our VIP client. She is labelled in our database as VIP. We've not only developed a friendship with her, but we've made her and her family a huge part of our team. Patty and her family get invited to all of our VIP events. If there's a cost associated with it, we waive the cost for them.

Since we've worked with Patty, almost four years ago, she has sent us five referrals. Three of those five referrals were both buy and sell. Now, any Real Estate Agent knows how incredibly powerful it is to be able to help not only with the purchase but the sale of the home, as well. If you do the math, those three deals were actually six. How do you put a value on someone like Patty in your database? I've mentioned how hard it is to look at people in terms of commission, but the reality of it is that it is so important for us to see the Patty's in our database and to see the value for every referral Patty sends us. This is where I go back to the training event and ask, "Do I know the value of my team's database?" So, moving forward, I will forever remember Patty and the value she adds to our database.

How do you see the value in that one client, and the business that they referred you? You take your Average Commission and you multiply that by how many referrals she has sent, that turned into closed deals. I'm just going to do it as the five transactions. So, let's say the Average Commission is $10,000. Multiply that by five closed referrals sent, and that equals $50,000 worth of Gross Commission Income (GCI) from one particular client. I don't know about you, but that is a client I want to keep happy and in constant contact with. I would want to keep track of the value she brings to our database.

If you look at that, in terms of volume, we're talking millions of dollars in volume. I'm not even talking about the buys and the sells from the three of those clients she referred. I'm just focused on Patty's referrals. Knowing the value of the database sets you apart from the average Agent and Administrator. If you haven't done this yet, start now. Go to your database, find your repeat and referral clients, and figure out their value. Call them, thank them for trusting you, and then write down how much business they have given you.

Patty gets invited to everything we do. We are so excited when she comes, and that has nothing to do with the fact that she's probably going to send more business our way, and everything to do with the relationship we've built with her. She trusts us so much to send her friends, family and strangers our way. She doesn't even flinch at that idea. You all need a Patty. Go to your database and find your Patty.

Having a great 8x8 system is another step in the right direction, as well. This famous 8x8 are the touches you will do with your clients when you initially put them in the database. Many of your clients should be set up to an ad campaign. Most databases and CRMs have campaign options. An 8x8 is broken down into calls, texts and emails. Market reports can be included in that, as well. Create your own 8x8. I'm going to give you an example of a very basic 8x8 that you can possibly implement into your business.

As you grow, you're going to expand that 8x8. There are a lot of teams out there right now doing anywhere from thirty-three to thirty-six touches, so it's possible that you can take an 8x8 and scale it. Where do you start? When I say touches, I'm referring to thirty-three touches over a one-year period, or eight touches over an eight-week period. The minute your client goes into the database, they should be set up to this campaign. Once in the database, that marketing campaign should instantly connect to them. They should start seeing your emails, start getting your phone calls, your text messages, whatever you've set up for your plan.

I can think of a quick top three for you to get started as an 8x8 flow idea. Number one is email blasts; number two is mailouts; number three is community events. So, when they're in the database, and you have them set up, they will automatically get all of your marketing material.

The following is an example of a high-level database with over 4,000 people in it. You do not need a heavy database to do this. This is a major key piece in having an effective database and controlling it; not having it control you. Determine your client level. This is where I'm going to go into more detail of your As, Bs and Cs and what they mean. As are typically zero to three months out for a purchase. Your Bs are typically four to six months out, and your Cs are seven to twelve months out. Why is that important? It's just really good to know how you will communicate with each person.

Your As are probably in the middle of looking or selling their homes with you or in contract negotiation. You are pretty much talking to them on a daily basis. These people will also be creating your referral pipeline because of the amazing job you've done with them. They will be set up to every campaign you are running. We will get to campaigns and 8x8s. I know I keep referring to them, I promise you we will go into detail, but first we need to establish the foundation around your database management.

Bs can sometimes be my favourite because they can jump to *A*s, in no time, and they are always happy to hear from you. The value they get from each call is amazing. They're in the stages of getting ready. Possibly seeking preapprovals and getting all their ducks in a row, which means they're ready, and will move into an A spot as soon as they can make that experience that much better for you, and them. Bs will be invited to all your campaigns. You want to keep them wanting more so that way you always stay top-of-mind with them. All it takes is missing one follow-up call with them and they could potentially go and work with somebody else. So how often do you follow-up with a B in your database? That's another great question we often get asked. Every three weeks is ideal—so they're not sick of you but they're also not hearing from you too much. One thing to keep in mind is that every conversation you have you are documenting it in your CRM notes, and setting the next reminder before you close down. If there is any indication of a change in their voice, change the follow-up to be more or less. Depending on the conversation, you have the control and the power to do that. Over communicating can be key, sometimes.

Cs need to stay top-of-mind, as well, as they are further out from purchasing and can switch gears quickly. This could be a missed opportunity if you miss a scheduled follow-up. Cs can be anywhere from two to three months out for a follow-up. A follow-up means phone calls and a personal touch to them. It doesn't mean that they're not getting everything that comes from the team in terms of marketing, it just means you also need to ensure you're putting phone calls in place to reach out and stay connected. Cs are invited to all of the basic stuff you and your team do. Your email blasts, newsletters, etc., so that you are always staying in front of them and not bombarding them too much.

As we begin to wrap up chapter six, I want to thank you so much for hanging in there. I know, each chapter is full of a lot of information and oftentimes, I will double dip and continuously talk about the same thing over and over again, I just really want to reiterate the importance of a strong database and how it is the bloodline of your business.

We've talked about As, Bs, and Cs in your database, the value in your database. We touched on 8x8 campaigns and a touch system. Remember to build out your database. The work you put in at the beginning will be absolutely worth it, I promise you this will help put your database on autopilot—outside of the regular phone calls you need to make. I'm going to be honest with you; when I talk about the database, I sometimes feel I lose people in the conversation because a lot of people don't feel it's important and they think, "I've got them in my phone, and I know when I need to call them." The reality of it is when you're working with an Administrator—your Empire Builder—and you're building a business, it is *not* okay that you do *not* put your notes in the CRM. Best advice I can give you is to put all communication into your CRM so that way, if you ever need your Administrator to pick up the phone and call the client, they know where you left off.

I feel it is so important for every business to really have your Administrator focus on the database to set them up for success. We've touched on the importance of contacts in the database —what a great example of being able to send an email blast and note cards to your clients. So, you're constantly top-of-mind. You can do that with a very detailed database, one that you can focus on and expand on while putting the plan in place to feed the database. Have your Admin go back to this chapter, or to every Empire Builder reading this chapter right now, I want you to go back to the beginning and research your database using this chapter. Understand the worth that's in the database and the value of each client in there. Do the referral and repeat business challenge I gave you earlier in this chapter, and know how much repeat and referral business you've done with particular clients.

To my Empire Builders, build your own database within your team's database. Imagine the power that your own personal database holds for the team. Challenge yourself to add twenty of your own contacts to the database—family, friends, people in your community. You can grow it together. It's important that you have a CRM you can grow. And I imagine you want one that can function at a high level. So do your research and don't just settle. If you currently have a database that you're working with, give it a try and don't give up on it. Just make sure it has all the functions we have discussed in this book.

Chances are, now that you've read this chapter, you haven't been giving it a good go. There's no need to switch databases if you don't need to. I've been there. Our team has done it. It's not fun. We simply upgraded our database. As our team grew, our CRM couldn't maximize all the things that we needed it to do. That is the only reason we moved into a new CRM. So do your research, look at some top databases in the Real Estate industry. Ask some of your peers what they are using. Take the time to research it. Once you have that CRM, have your

Admin watch the training videos so they are one step ahead of you and they're able to teach you some of the tips, or tricks and tools, when on-boarding Agents.

Empire Builders, one of the most important commitments you need from your Agents moving forward is that they will utilize the database and set every client up for success, every day. So, it goes back to leading by example. You commit to using it at a high level, that way there is no option for your Agent. This will be the most powerful tool you can offer an Agent outside of your leadership; knowing all things CRM and database related.

Okay, it's time for another quick game. Let's say you have 320 contacts in your database. Multiply that by your Average Commission . . . I can wait. Think about that number. That's how many dollars are sitting in your database right now. It should make you want to pick up the phone and give them all a call. That makes you want to know the details of your database, your follow-ups, and your reminders. That's the power in your database right now, that number. Imagine if you had a database of 2,000 people. Kind of makes you want to close this book up and go work on that database, doesn't it? Don't do that just yet. There is a lot more good stuff coming your way.

To my Admins, here comes your challenge. I really want to make you the next Empire Builder for your business. Make sure the correct information is going into the database, if it isn't already. I then want you to plan a day, it may even take two days depending on the size of your database, where you can go through and ensure that every client in there has a reminder for a follow-up call. If you see a note from your Agent in a clients' account where it says, "Wants me to call them in three months," look at that date, see how far out it is, and make sure that an accurate reminder is in there for the Agent. Create the 8x8 campaign and use the example that I shared with you; it's a popular one. Many teams utilize this so I can't take credit for creating it, but I can take credit for the success it's given our team.

Starting right now you must ensure that every contact entered is correct. Set yourself up for success by labelling your database. Whether it's a past client or a referral client, make sure every client has a label because it elevates the level of care, the interaction and client experience. Don't forget to add your twenty contacts to the database, daily. I mean you; my Empire Builders can feed the database. I'm asking you to commit to feeding the database. That's it! That is our database chapter in a nutshell. I cannot wait to hear your successes from this chapter.

SIMPLE 8x8 TO SET UP DATABASE

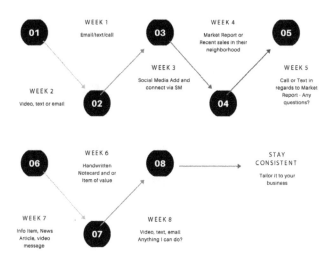

CHAPTER 7

EFFECTIVE SYSTEMS

for Client Experience

This chapter will teach you how to create effective listing and buyer systems to take your Agent to the next level in client experience. As we jump into chapter seven, the one thing I want to express is just how incredibly important this chapter will be to your Administrator. We have laid the basic foundation for a team. We've talked about the communication database. We are going to dive deep into systems and models, and, really, I'm going to give you one system that you can use today to build on. This is where you will leverage your Admin for absolute success. We will talk about our listing systems and models, in general, but we will start with the foundation for a great solid listing system.

We're going to talk about creating an effective listing and buyer system to take your Agent to the next level in client experience. I'm going to break down some important systems for you that you may have already tried, or already heard of, that possibly didn't work out. I have this motto: Don't give up on a system until the system has proven to fail you. Often, we don't even let it take its course to get to that point because we jumped ship. After all, it's hard work and I'll be honest, there are a lot of Agents who probably haven't had an Admin, so it's been an incredible workload and adding to it isn't something you want to do. You want to be able to go get the deal, get out and service the clients.

You have an Administrator now, so you can elevate your level of business and there is no better system to do this than the listing system. What we've talked about before is the basic foundations of building a Real Estate business. Now we're talking about that system. I'm going to give you a few points on how to build a successful listing business system. It all starts in your presentation. Having a strong presentation, when you go on your appointments, sets the bar far above anybody else. It shows them that you're here for them; that you've created a business and this isn't just a one-off for you. It's important that you understand the value of a great listing presentation and that this team provides so much more value to your clients.

Let's gain some clarity around this. How does the Admin help build this presentation and support the Agent with the appointments? We're going to start off at the point where you have booked the appointment and you're ready to go on your listing appointment. It's a conversation you have with your Admin, now. In my world, as Operations, we prep the file, which includes all the presentation material and the listing paperwork. We do two types of listing paperwork: Exclusive Period & Regular Listing Period. I'm going to talk a little bit more about exclusive periods, as we get going, but understanding how to prep a file is the only thing that we don't do for our Agents because this is where your research comes in. Your homework is getting to know your clients and your client's neighbourhood, so that's why you pull your comps in that respective neighbourhood and work on the geo warehouse.

A lot of people don't think of utilizing such an undervalued tool. For us, it's a tool we use daily for everything we do. Pulling the geo warehouse and knowing how to read a geo report. Not every client's going to want you to go through it all with them as it's quite a large document. That's where you identify what type of client you have, where you could maybe leave the geo at their house, or for some you, could go through it with a fine-toothed comb with them. Whichever method you choose to do, don't do it for you; do it for your client. Read your client and know who will want you to read it or who's going to want you to leave it.

Admins, you want to set the Agent up for success. If they don't already have a nice folder and a presentation for listings, I want you to create one. There are a lot of tools and methods you can use, such as Canva, to create a nice listing presentation. It will boil down to marketing because all the things that we've talked about up until now will be intricate to your listing system. Just being able to document and share your social media reach, alone, and making your client aware of this in the presentation package is a powerful piece of marketing info. Not only do you have a strong database that you will use to reach so many people, via email blasts, but you also have a social media outreach and can gain anywhere from ten to 75,000 views on your current listings, weekly. Know that number.

It all comes down to being able to track it at a high level. Do you see how every chapter is kind of tying in with one another? Create a listing presentation that talks about the benefits of working with you and your team. Create branding around it. Have tips and suggestions for when they list. Prepare and have all listing materials right at your Agents' fingertips. If you are stuck on what information you put into your listing pamphlets, there are a lot of materials online. Whatever you are going to use from the internet, make sure it fits your brand. Have an eye-catching presentation folder that you can use to present your material. How you show up at this appointment is how your clients will think you show up during the process, so please show up at your absolute best.

Let's go back for a minute. If you go into an appointment empty-handed, is that how you'll show up for them? Throughout the process, Admins, I want you to look at what the listing presentation is right now and if you're confident it will be the best you've ever seen, and then keep going. If there's anything else that you could be adding to it, please do. Look like you're a million-dollar Real Estate Agent. Use good quality paper.

The upfront cost will be worth it. Make sure you include listing and exclusive paperwork, here's why: During the listing presentation, you go in confidently and have a conversation with them, even if they might not be ready to list. They may be two weeks away due to some small things they need to do to get ready to list. Imagine if you could still market their property for them while they're getting ready to sell it. This way, when they're ready to go, you've already been able to have showings on it. Through social media, gain interest in traction and it will sell faster for them.

Having the seller sign an exclusive paperwork period might set you apart from a lot of the other Agents. I'm getting ahead of myself here because I am missing some key things I want to talk about, but I feel like this is one thing where your mind will be blown. These systems are so incredible for building successful listings for your team. Not only do I want to talk about the geo warehouse and exclusive listings, but I also want to talk to you about a listing timeline. This is going to be essential.

It took us a long time to make this tool as successful as it is for us today. As we grew, we were more confident in our conversations with our clients. We made changes to the timeline based on their feedback. We will never perfect this, and we will always be changing and updating our listing timeline. It's a graph, and the graph represents the timeline from signed paperwork to first Open House. So, what happens before the photographer comes? What happens after the photographer leaves? When do we email our database to showcase our new listing? Our exclusive period, does it need to be staged? If so, what part of the timeline is staging in there? The timeline is from the moment of the appointment to the time we do our first Open House. We leave that listing timeline with our clients so they always have it in front of them, and it eliminates any kind of questions or lingering thoughts they forgot to ask. They can always refer to the timeline and say, "Oh, Tuesday is photos. Thursday, we go live. Sunday is our Open House . . ." for example. This has probably been one of the key pieces in our listing presentation and is one of the most successful tools we've implemented.

I want to move to the next part. Your listing presentation was next to none. You were able to go in there and confidently talk about how many views their home will get with your online presence and how many people you have in your database. You can get in touch with other Agents in your community. How many listings you sold last year? How many days on the market? You gave them all the information; they never had to second guess how confident this decision would be to hire you to sell their home. I always say for those of us who charges anywhere from the 5 percent to 6 percent range, we better bring that value. We better make sure that we replace that percentage with the ultimate client experience, and I feel very strongly about that. You get what you pay for.

You've crushed the appointment, and now you're ready to move to the next step. There are so many things in between the moment you leave the appointment to the moment you get back to the office. Maybe you forgot what day you told them to do photos, or what day we are going to have a stager come in, or do we need a cleaning company to go in? So many things are going on in that appointment. It's okay to feel that way. It's not okay, though, to lose that information before you get back to your Admin.

You're probably asking yourself, "Is she going somewhere with this?" I am. Again, I have to give credit to an amazing class that I took four years ago. There was one sheet of paper that this lady said she used when she would come back from her listing appointments. This piece of paper held all the power to move forward and she thought this was the best method to communicate with her clients, and her Admin. She called it, "Pass the Baton." It's just one sheet of paper with all the info needed. I took that lesson, and I created a sheet that's tailored to our team.

During the meeting with the client, our Agents have it open. That's where our listing Agents write their notes. It talks about what type of client we are dealing with, and we use what's called the DISC profile through Tony Robbins. It's a tool that helps identify personalities and is a great tool to learn how to communicate with our clients. When the Admins call the client, we now know how to better communicate with them based on the DISC profile in the Pass the Baton.

This is our communication tool between our Agent and Admin. The Agent will tuck it into the folder, bring the folder back to the office, and hand it to the Admin. Now, Agents, please don't hate me for what's about to come. We have a strict rule on our team that if there's anything blank on the paperwork, such as initials weren't filled out or the communication tool wasn't filled out properly, we won't touch the file. We call the client, and here's why: You should never be calling a client and saying, "I'm so sorry, 'so and so,' I forgot about this at your appointment. I'm going to have to send this back over to you to sign." You have to set the bar high, especially when you're taking 5 percent to 6 percent interest. You want to go in there and get the information you need because you want to excel at that first impression and set the Admin up for success.

Imagine having your Admin not receive all the key things that you've discussed with the client—we don't know if we are staging, we don't know what the live date is. We're not really running a business this way. There's nothing fun about that, and there's nothing fun about calling a client to say that we forgot this and/or that.

Actually, we will not even look at the file. We'll fold it back up, congratulate the Agent on getting the listing, and then we give the file back to the Agent. You're probably wondering, "Why hire an Admin if their making you do all this work." We're relationship based, and I want to point that out. Everything we do comes down to how we build a strong relationship with our client. We give the file back to the Agent for them to make that call. Having your Admin make that call for you doesn't make you look like a strong listing Agent. It makes you look like a person who has people to do things for you.

When you're connecting with your client, they don't know about team dynamics and they don't know about how an Admin works behind the scenes. They know you, and that is why we have the Agents call them back. When you do this, you're not just building rapport with them; you're building rapport for repeat and referral business. Therefore, you must complete all the information and bring the file back, 100 percent completed, to get started on listing the property.

What I want you all to do is, take a minute and think about a communication tool that you can be using that will set your team apart and keep strong communication flowing between you, your Admin, and your client. Because, at this point, your Admin is probably going to be doing a lot of the setup of the listing—calling the client to book everything, getting contact information, making sure it's accurate for showings, lockbox pick-ups/drop-offs, etc. We are going to need strong communication and it's going to need to have a tool in place.

Just a quick little piece on the communication tool, some really good ideas to have on that would be the listing date you've decided on with the client. Did you leave the listing timeline at their house, so they understand? Do they need staging? Do they need photography? Do they need cleaning, and if so, when can we do this? What is left to do? Do they need our vendor's list?

As we grow together, I will be able to share with you the steps to hold your Agent accountable to these systems as well, because, on the flip side, we know that it's going to be our job to implement it. That's an important part of the process and is where the relationship and the building of trust come into play. The only thing the Agent should be doing after this appointment, and making sure the paperwork is correct, is following up with the client to let them know some pivotal moments that are about to happen, such as, when their live date is, calling to check-in and follow-up; the Admin has everything else under control.

One quick little story before I move on. When it was just my Agent and I, we would get so excited going on a listing appointment because it meant there was momentum, and that we were helping someone new. We were super excited and he loved getting in front of clients talking about our systems. He had a great presentation in place. Every year we would take in the feedback that we'd received from clients around their listing experience, determined how we could be better, and we would continue adding to the tool.

For every listing appointment he would go on, I would leave a little inspirational or motivational Post-it note on top of his file, or sometimes I'd be funny and say, "If you don't get this listing, don't come back to the office," or, "You got this, so go in there, charm them, and let them know you're here for them." Anything that we could pick up about the client, and I would leave little fun notes in the file so that when he got to the appointment, or in the car before the appointment, he could see those little Post-it notes. I was hoping that it would excite him again and remind him that we're in this together and that he's not doing this alone.

So, if there's anything that you can think of that you can add for your Agent to build momentum and create a little experience for the both of you, do it. Build trust with yourselves and a relationship in the process. Remember, at the end of this, you're not just listing a home; you're helping a family move to the next step in their life, whatever that looks like. This isn't just a sale. As you grow and you do more listings, sometimes it does become routine. I want you always to stop and remember that every person you meet contributes to your growth, no matter how many listing appointments you go on.

A quick tip before we move on; for those listing appointments that you don't get (I don't like putting that out into the environment, but it does happen), ensure you let your Admin know and schedule reminder calls to call the client to get feedback on how you could have done better. It sounds silly, I know, and many people think why would we need to do that? It's really important to understand that some of your growth opportunities come from feedback, good or bad. Therefore, we accept the feedback, grow from it, and get the next listing.

If the Agent is set up correctly for success, in my mind, the only thing an Agent should be doing is pulling comps and researching the neighbourhood, and home, before they go. If you are going into an appointment with empty hands, that will change from this moment on.

Create a listing presentation that talks about the benefits of working with you and brand it to match your team branding. When they list, offer tips and suggestions on how to prepare their home. All this stuff is right at your fingertips on the internet. Have a sleek folder that you use for presenting your material.

Remember, how you show up at this appointment is how you show up during the showing. Now you've come back from the listing appointment and, without a doubt, your Agent got it! Place a follow-up call for the next day to ensure there are no questions unanswered and let them know you will also be sending a digital copy of the listing and exclusive paperwork to them that afternoon.

Key Tip to Start Now

Create a communication tool for you and your Agent. A piece of paper tucked into the folder with all the info needed to set you and your Agent up for the ultimate client experience. On that sheet should be the list date. Have a mini calendar on it. Have a listing timeline that you can also leave with your client. Do they need staging? Do they know when a photographer is coming? Gather as much info, as needed, to start the listing process.

To my Empire Builders, as we grow together, I will share with you steps to hold your Agent accountable to these systems. The most important part is setting up the listing, booking a photographer and coordinating times with the client.

Reminder: At this point, the only thing the Agent should be doing is following up with the client. Check-in and let them know pivotal moments that will be happening with their live date.

Now the listing is live and the fun begins. Have a proposal for Open House, etc. Set yourself up as a business. Now we go into what is called marketing the listing. You have a few options here, so bear with me as we jump back and forth. During the exclusive period, you can market the listing as, "Coming Soon," on social media. It's gone live on MLS, so you can use headings, such as, "NEW LISTING," or, "Open House this Weekend." Boosting these on social media will gain brand awareness and leads, as well. To get this house sold, your job, as an Admin, is to make sure you have a marketing plan in place and a system for leads as they come through.

Open Houses

Let's talk about leveraging the listing. We're going to go right into the Open House system next, I promise. Anyone can put a sign in front of a house and advertise an Open House, but what are you going to do differently to separate yourself from the rest? That's what this book is really about. It's to get you from point A to point B, faster. I'm sharing with you successes that I've experienced myself. I have gone to an Open House, just to see how other Agents interact with clients or how they run an Open House. I suggest doing it in a virtual world now, as a lot of people are doing virtual Open Houses online.

I encourage you to watch other Agents' virtual videos, and how they're doing it. What are you going to do to be one step ahead? The most important thing in Real Estate is taking the systems you have, moving to the next part of it, and to be constantly growing it. I just want to pause and bring some attention to what exactly the listing does for you at this point, not the client:

- Free marketing to generate more leads
- Open House/marketing the Open House—more opportunity to lead-generate
- Sign on the lawn to attract neighbours
- Opportunity to cold-call the neighbourhood—new listing in your neighbourhood
- Door-knocking to invite people to your Open House

And last, but not least, branding your name in the community. I did mention a few different marketing techniques because there are so many different methods you can use to market this. I listed five major things, and you could probably condense a couple, but I couldn't help myself because listings are an amazing tool towards the growth of your business, exposure in the community and access to reach thousands of people. It's how you market yourself and take advantage of the opportunity that can potentially separate you from the rest.

Open House Systems

Do you have an Open House system? Do you feel confident in the system you have that you'll be able to generate leads? Or, generate social media momentum and attract homeowners, and/or buyers, to your Open House? Open Houses can be one of the best tools. During a listing presentation, or a listing, sit somewhere for two hours and have leads come to you. I mean, does it get any better than that? Not just having a system of showing up and waiting for people to come in the door. What are you going to do to set the bar high and create a system like no other, and are you prepared to do that?

You can absolutely take your Open House tools to the next level and I'm going to share some tools of success for you around Open Houses.

Our team typically starts our Open House systems on a Friday (we often do a Saturday and Sunday Open House) and typically finish all things related to Open Houses on a Monday, after our follow-ups and marketing are completed. We don't look at Open House systems just as an Open House, an opportunity to sit for a couple of hours and have a break from the hustle and bustle, hoping that a couple of people will come through the door. We spend our week setting this up for success. That way, while we're there we can focus on the people that walk through the door and get that house sold for our client.

If you track your numbers, you will know what your lead turnover is, your lead conversion on an Open House, how many clients come in that you were able to convert into your clients, or how many clients come in that are already working with another Agent. Those are good stats to look for. I'm going to talk a little bit below about our systems and our team. What we do to set the bar high, and how we set ourselves up and separate ourselves from all the others. We call it "Seventh Level Open Houses."

Set up an Open House system. Again, some Agents take years to perfect this and I am showing you a high-level system to get you to the top of your game faster. What will you do leading up to the Open House to build awareness and generate leads for you and your Agents? Virtual videos advertising the Open House, door-knocking, inviting the neighbours (they may have a friend or family member who wants to move to the area).

Write a list of three things a listing does for you, and then let's compare.

Okay, ready?

- Free marketing
- Lead funnel
- More marketing with an Open House
- Face-to-face with potential clients via an Open House

- Marketing opportunities
- Branding your name in that community

Okay, I went with six major things. A listing is an amazing tool towards growth for your business, exposure in communities, and the ability to reach thousands of people. It's how you market yourself and take advantage of the opportunities that separate you from the rest. Having a great Open House system is one of those great tools.

Sign-In Sheets: We turn people away if they do not sign-in. We make sure we protect our clients, and if that means turning those away that are unwilling to understand that, then that's okay. It's a high standard we hold for our clients. Our team does a live Open House video right before it starts, inviting any last-minute people when we can. Our Open Houses typically run from 2:00 p.m. until 4:00 p.m. However, our Agents don't stop working until after follow-ups are complete. It is what sets us apart from the average Agent. How do you do that?

After the Open House, we call or email everyone who is not working with an Agent to thank them for coming to our Open House and ask for any additional feedback. We immediately add those people to our database and add the appropriate reminder to their contact info. We also send them a personalized note card, thanking them again for coming. We don't stop our day until that's done. If anyone we spoke with is interested in a listing appointment, home evaluation, or is interested in looking at homes with us, we make sure we continue servicing them.

I'm hoping I didn't overwhelm anyone here. There is so much value in this chapter. If you don't see the importance of having a strong listing system for marketing, building brand awareness, getting new listings, leveraging your Admin to build a listing presentation for you and creating that experience behind the scenes, I want you to reread this chapter. There are some big takeaways here, and I'm sharing a lot of the secrets of our team's success. Well, they're not exactly secrets because we enjoy sharing some of the things that work well for us.

I'm scratching the surface because it's such a big system, but I want to make sure that I can give you some takeaways; some things to implement and, more importantly, how to leverage your Admin with your listing models.

Here's a quick story on my team's behalf. We track how many people come through the door during a listing or an Open House. How many people have an Agent, how many people don't? One thing that we believe in, firmly, is not calling clients who are assigned to other Agents. That's a big no-no. A lot of times during Open Houses, we don't know if they are working with another Agent. Having an effective system in place to get that information is helpful because one of the things you don't want to do is add people to your database that don't belong there.

Creating a culture within your Real Estate community means you don't want to be stepping on anyone's toes. It's not great business and, at the end of the day, it doesn't do much for your listing or your client.

I strongly feel that with listing systems, marketing systems and Open House systems go hand in hand for our team. I want you to look at your Open House system, and find some gaps where you can improve; what you can add and what you can take out? What you're doing is elevating the client experience, so they want to come to your Open House. What will you do that no one else is thinking of doing right now? Give any great ideas or any success stories. I'd love to hear them, so please find me on social media and share, or tag me in your Open House videos. I would love to see them all.

Take a minute and think about all the possibilities of a listing. Grab a pen and a piece of paper because I want you to write down three things that a listing does for you and then we're going to compare some notes.

Quick Tip: If you feel overwhelmed by the amount of information that I have given you, take notes, highlight specific parts, and/or bend the corner of the page to come back to it. This is a strong resource tool, and I want to remind everyone, you cannot implement everything you read here at once. More importantly, do take notes and give them to your Admin. Admins, if you are reading this, take notes and start thinking of the steps needed to implement the items you will create. I am also here to help in any way I can.

CHAPTER 8

MARKETING & BRANDING

All right, welcome to one of my favourite chapters: Marketing and Branding. It's one of my favourite things to do for our team. I'm going to talk about the basics of marketing and building the foundation in a platform. So, if there's anyone reading this who hasn't created that brand, or that marketing platform, or that social media, or community, then this is just going to be the basic steps to get started, especially if you've hired a new Admin.

Let's be honest, we don't hire Marketing Directors; we hire Executive Assistants. So, just keep in mind that a lot of us are jumping in and wearing multiple hats and learning on the fly. That's why it's important to hire Top Talent. If their resume says they have marketing experience, that's great. That's an asset, but don't shy away from people who don't have marketing experience because some people are very creative and, given an opportunity and an outlet to express that, can help bring out the unlocked potential in an Executive Assistant.

This is something that revitalizes me when I have the time to do marketing and create social media posts. This is my fun time of the day. I want to dedicate this chapter to marketing, branding and social media. Again, I want to remind you that I will be talking about the basics—the very first models and systems you should have in place. If you're already at this level, it's okay to read this because it might rejuvenate you in some areas. It also might show you where you need to up your game. If you've been in the industry for a long time and you're still just working at a basic level, and everything that I talked about is what you do every day, ask yourself this, "What am I going to do differently to elevate our marketing, branding and social media platforms?"

Marquee is a key piece that generates business brand exposure, lead-generator and community awareness. Having a great brand for your team can increase the appeal to the market. As well, it's important when you're creating your marketing platform to document it. I'm going to go into a quick story about marketing and branding on our team.

We've been using a very basic model for the last four years, and there's nothing wrong with that. We expand and we grow in certain areas of it, but the basic model is this: creating content and creating a timeline. From Monday to Friday, we know what posts are going out on our social media, our branding. We did a rebrand two years ago and it's used on all of our marketing material. Our marketing plans are well beyond an 8x8, and we are still doing many community events. You must follow the brand. You become the brand on your social media accounts. If you choose to keep your social media personality and not brand it to look like you are part of the team, then that's great. There's nothing wrong with that, but I will take you back to the first chapter where we talked about your worth and how to show your value. If people know you're in Real Estate, they'd be more apt to come to you as you build your brand awareness and your pipeline through your personal social media. You're going to wear multiple hats. You will be a social media expert, you will be a marketing and branding guru, and you will have fun doing it. It's fun to play around and be creative with events that are coming up.

I have never taken marketing and branding courses. My experience strictly comes from being given the opportunity with our team. Our team has built a recognizable brand within our community, and surrounding cities, with just one logo. It lets people know right off the bat that when they see it, they know who we are. It projects from our weekly mailouts and our email blasts to our banners, our Open House signs and our sold signs. One universal logo covers all of our marketing pieces, choosing a colour and a font that's vibrant, stands out, and is attractive to the eye.

I'm not going to go deep into marketing and branding with you because, to be honest, that's not my area of expertise and I want to keep this basic. I want to allow you to build a basic system and grow on it. Let me share some initial steps to get started. First, get all social media accounts up and running, immediately. Separate your Agents' accounts, so there is a business one and a personal one. If you intend to grow a team, I suggest a personal or business page dedicated to the team. It's going to set you up for long-term growth.

LinkedIn is booming right now and if you can post videos, this is a great area to work in. People are still testing the waters here, in some sense, in Real Estate and, if you can master LinkedIn, it will be a great asset in your social media platform. Facebook has been a huge asset to our team and Real Estate. You can drop posts, reviews, and create events for Open Houses; driving brand exposure. Instagram is a great platform to build your brand, your stories, and it's a way to set the bar high for you and your Agent.

Let's backtrack a little bit. LinkedIn is a great tool for recruiting. It's appealing to bigger audiences in more of a business perspective. Create a Facebook group and add people to that group, share and create events and Open Houses, too. Instagram is more for your story. You can showcase certain things like what the team looks like, how we operate, sharing stories and personal successes. It focuses more on the person and the team than it does on the selling and the buying. People feel more comfortable to reach out to us and ask us about upcoming listings. We generate quite a bit of business from our Instagram and Facebook accounts. There, your first step is creating your basic social media accounts. If you haven't already done some branding or a logo, which will spread all across your media outlets and email signatures, etc., this should be the first thing on your list. Branding is key! It's a way for everyone in your community to recognize you.

After all your accounts are set up and your branding has been initiated, start inviting your friends, family and clients to like and/or follow your social media pages. Use the listing timeline you've created to know how to create a calendar of content, for example: Live Tuesdays, Live Thursdays, or Open House Fridays. You can highlight your Agents on the team by creating informative videos. There is so much content right at your fingertips.

Instagram, as I said, is a more behind the scenes platform. You can share the listings with the buyers, but people want to see you and what you guys are doing. It's a great way to build the brand for your Agent. This could be a great tool for recruiting, as well. As you grow this platform, whatever method you choose you have to start documenting the system, decide on lead funneling, and, more importantly, boost ads. It's important for whatever system you implement.

Analyzing Social Media

Now, we are going to jump into the fun part of Facebook—the analysis part, the boosting your ads part; all the stuff to extend your reach into the community and the social media world. Remember, I'm going to go back and say this again; whatever you do, document your systems. I made a mistake as I was growing our team by not documenting the systems as I went and I had to sit down and spend months coming up with an Operations Manual. Documenting your systems from the very beginning will help you long-term. Trust me, I'm speaking from experience.

Facebook Manager is a great tool, it will boost ads through Facebook and it will allow you to cross share with Instagram. If people click on your boosted post and inquire for more information, make sure you have a call to action as an easy way for a potential client to reach out to you. Have a system around boosting your ads. I'm going to give you a little bit of experience because the reason why I feel strongly about making sure this is in the book is the fact that this is where you could lose potentially hundreds of dollars within your marketing budget.

I'm going to share this with you from an experience that I've had. Boosting ads costs money and you want to see your reach, who your clientele is, what community you want to target and all of that stuff. A lot of people will pay a $100 here and a $100 there, or $50 here and $50 there. But, before you know it, you're spending $500, or more, for one listing and three posts, and that's not really beneficial.

The idea is that the more money you can invest into your social media targeted ads, the more potential for gaining leads. I think you will get a little bit more attention by doing this, but is it the right attention? We've been very purposeful with our targeted ads. When we're boosting ads, we have our target audience in specific areas that we're looking for. We don't spend more than $25 per boost. So, let's jump back to the exclusive listings I was talking about in the listing systems chapter, for a minute. We boost an exclusive post when it goes live. Possibly a week later, we boost it for another $25 for the upcoming Open House. And then, we boost it a final time, for $25, when sold. Be very purposeful with your budget in marketing, especially if you plan to carry multiple listings.

Suppose you're a heavy listing Agent, which is amazing, great, high-five to you! I love that. You're listing anywhere from one to sixteen properties. You have to be very purposeful with where your ad dollars go. Now, with that being said, we've listed multiple million-dollar homes and some over the million-dollar mark. We know we need to reach more people, and our area of reach needs to be bigger. We invest $75 on the live post and $25 on the exclusive post.

We talked about social media basics—just scraping the surface—leading us to our database and how we reach our database. This also ties in with your 8x8 and email blasts. Once we list a property and post it on social media, we send out an email blast to our database, introducing our new listing. This is also a key value piece in our listing presentation. Letting our clients know how much exposure they will get working with our team, explaining that the reach we have on our social media platform spans from 600–10,000 views each week, which is giving the client even more exposure to getting the listing SOLD.

Email blast, newsletter, and database marketing are great opportunities to set your Agent up for success and build a massive presence. Email blasts are a basic, non-intrusive way to stay in touch with your current clients. If they are in the database, you have connected with them at some point, or at least that is a good reason for them being in there.

HOT TIP: Database Marketing

I'm going to share a small tip that many of us don't listen to. Do not just add people to your database for the sake of growing it. You're just doubling your work time, and there is no real value to your database. Over the years, we have grown to realize it's about who's in there, not how many I can add. When you have that mindset, you tend to have a messy database that will take weeks to correct. Start on the right foot to build a valuable database and clientele.

Tracking

All right, so we've talked about boosting our post and creating a marketing platform; a small basic system to get us started. We're going to jump into why tracking is important. Admins, I want you to add this to your list of things to do. For every post that you boost, I want you to research and track the stats behind it. How many people clicked on it? How many people shared it? How many people commented on it? Facebook manager will give you all of that information. It will give you data analysis on the post that you have boosted. If you're cross-posting it with Instagram, it will do the same thing.

The reason why I say it is important to track, plain and simple, is that it saves you a lot of time and energy from the things that are not working well, and focuses you on the ones that are working well. For example, you would think that your listings are the most popular posts you put up there when, in reality, it was an Open House video you did on the property or a market report video you shared. You'd be surprised to see what people watch. The only way you'll know is if you track it.

Here's another reason why I feel strongly about tracking. You can take this information and use it during your listing appointment. Put it in your listing presentation paperwork.

Share what your database reaches, how many people view your post and how many followers you have. It shows your clients, when you're listing their properties, the leverage you have, the competence you have, and the exposure can you provide. You will get their house listing. Many people don't think of that tool during a listing appointment, and it's almost like it doesn't matter to a lot of people, nowadays. It is one of the top questions asked by clients; how are you going to promote us on social media? What do you do differently than other people?

I want you to stop and ask yourself those questions. What do you do differently on the social media platforms that separate you from the rest? What could you be doing differently to elevate that level of service? We're just really scraping the surface here. I feel like I'm struggling, holding myself back from going deeper into marketing and branding, because in this world we live in right now, it is a very virtual based world and I want us all to be comfortable manoeuvring through it. Just remember there's no right or wrong way of doing things. It's just important to have a very basic foundation and be able to identify if something isn't working and move on.

If anyone's reading this who is very uncomfortable putting themselves out on social media, that's okay. Many Agents hide behind their listings and their posts, and choose not to do videos of current events. They would much rather send that information out during an email blast, and that's fine. I just want you to understand the potential opportunities you are missing out on by not putting yourself out there.

On the flip side, Admins, I'm challenging you to push your Agent outside of their comfort zone; good things happen out there, growth happens out there. I know many people say, "Oh no, Realtors love to get in front of a camera. They love it when people are taking photos and they're doing videos." Yes, there are many of us out there who are very comfortable doing that stuff, but there's also a few of us that need to be pushed to do it. Getting out there on social media is the way of the world now. We're living in a virtual world where if you can't get face-to-face with people, get your face on a screen where people can see you, hear your voice, and relate to who you are. That's great branding.

One little tip I'm going to give you about social media is to always be true to yourself. I'm a very open and honest person. I don't like it when people pretend to be something else so that people will like them, or get business from being a certain way. Be genuine. Be authentic. That's what's going to attract people to you. If you're someone who has a little bit of a negative mindset, figure out how to change the way you look at things. Don't write complaining posts on your social media. People are watching, and nobody wants to work with those people. Stay positive and stay true to yourself.

Suppose you are someone who likes to rant about politics on Facebook. I'm just going to suggest maybe writing it out on a piece of paper instead of going to Facebook. That way, you get the feelings out but you're not sharing them with the public. One of the unfortunate parts is how we are portrayed and how people see us. Real Estate Agents struggle with people not knowing just how real and how amazing you can be, and how hard you work. Don't give them more fuel to think that you're any less of a person and give them something to call you out on for diminishing the value you bring to your social media.

Email List Marketing

I'm about to blast you with the basic steps of marketing methods. I'm not talking about social media for the moment; I am moving on to other marketing techniques. A few chapters back we touched on the database. The 8x8 campaign is another strong system to have in place, as well as email blasts. Having a strong database is amazing; having an incredible email list is even more amazing. I'm going to spend the next part of the chapter talking about some methods our team uses once we list a property and post it on social media.

After the social media posts, we send out our email blast. On top of the 10,000 to 20,000 people we've reached through our social media, we're also getting out to the 9,000 in our database. This is giving the client even more exposure. It's reiterating to them what you said in your listing presentation about how far your reach can grow.

Getting the client more exposure and getting the listing sold—isn't that your goal? On the positive side, it will attract more opportunities for new listings. Another major factor in your marketing is having a top-of-the-line photographer. This is an incredible asset to your team. If you are at an average style marketing level and charging a high commission, I'm going to challenge you to seek out a talented photographer who will give you an over-the-top marketing and branding experience—one that sets you apart from all the other Agents. This is a major game-changer for our team. Our listing photos are a huge part of our marketing and branding.

Now, I'm going to jump into a little something here. Our photographer creates 3D tours, photos, videos using drones, night tours and creates a personalized website for each of our listings, but it comes at a cost. The talent in our photographer is incredible and worth every penny. Having a good photographer will set you apart from everybody else. Marketing isn't all social media; it's in your brand. It's how you portray yourself and how you market yourself as a Real Estate Agent. Our photographer is not a member of our team, he is an outside vendor. However, we only work with like-minded individuals, so it goes back to our culture again. Our photographer matches our culture. Seek the value in adding these small little touches to your business. It makes a huge impact and people notice.

Now, we'll jump back to the email blasts. Let's break down the opportunity to build a strong foundation here:

New Listings: I will use our team as an example. Every Tuesday an email blast is sent announcing our new listings, a photo, and basic info included, with a call to action at the bottom.

Open Houses: Every Friday we send out our email titled: Open Houses this Weekend.

Email Blast: Listing all of our virtual and in-person Open Houses, welcoming all to come. For the virtual Open House, we include the links to see us online and get your private showing. This has been a massive success to our team and usually generates the most responses.

Market Stats: Every month your Real Estate board will send out the stats for your neighbourhood and surrounding area. We compile this info, brand it to our team, and blast it out via email and social media. This monthly blast has been a permanent fixture for our team for four years. It is a key piece of information. If we ever miss sending this, our clients know and contact us to make sure we send it.

These email blasts may have put some of you in panic mode because it sounds like a huge commitment. It is a huge commitment, but it's also a template we completed four years ago and it takes minutes to put together now. The first few times it takes work to put it together, but you are setting up your future self for success. These email blasts take minutes to create and seconds to send out. The work is so worth it. Do the work and commit to it. I promise there is a massive payout to these email blasts.

In this chapter, your homework is to create a system around one of the email blast options I have given you. Don't try to do them all. That's not setting yourself up for success. If your agency currently has an email blast going, make sure it's branded and bringing value with it. You could then choose another one to implement if you have mastered your Agent's first email blast. There is no race to have all of these at the same time. This is your growth pace, so don't rush yourself. You will get to this level in no time. One of the important necessities with social media and building a system around marketing is having a strong foundation for correspondence, engagement, and leads. I promise you, with a concrete system, leads will come. Our marketing and branding generate over 35 percent of our leads for our team.

Engagement Tip: So, let us stop for a minute because we all know we will have our online haters; those who think you've overpriced the home or had a bad experience (even if they didn't work with you). This happens, and we thank those people for responding and we ask them if there is anything else we can do to help them out. They don't get ignored, but they also don't go unanswered. We appreciate all comments and suggestions.

Return on Investment

Yes! We made it. We made it through the marketing and branding part of this book and, like I said, we just scraped the surface. There's so much more to dabble in here. If this isn't an area of expertise for you or your Administrator, seek an outside marketing company to consult with you and put a plan in place, starting by building an email list. One of the most important things about social media branding, and building a system around marketing, is having that strong foundation for correspondence and engaging the leads that come through. We talked about this a little bit before.

Admins, you will have leads coming through social media. Who's in charge of that? If it's just you and your Agent, I would say that's the Agent's job. That would be part of their lead-gen. If they are able to time block a set amount of time to answer social media leads, and be able to handle that lead right away, conversion will be higher. As your team grows, this won't be scalable to have your Agents focus solely on all of the leads that come through. This is when you might have to step in, where, through the day, you time block to make sure you're answering any comments and questions that people have on the social media platform. Then after hours, your Agent takes it over.

I'm going to share a funny story with you. My husband hates when I share this story for obvious reasons. I've been with our team for years. I've said that before. In the last four years, we've generated this brand within our community and the cities surrounding us. We have people from Vancouver who reach out to us, from the US who reach out to us, and want us to help them find vacation properties here in Ontario. We're everywhere! We are firm believers in getting as much content out as you can, as long as it has value and targets the right people. What are you doing right now to build an over-the-top marketing experience? And, do you know what your return on this investment looks like?

So, I have two stories, but let me finish my first story. Again, I'm going down a rabbit hole here. My husband was in a grocery store, and he ran into one of his high school friends. I didn't go to high school with my husband; we met after that. I'm not even from the same area as him. So, he bumped into one of his friends from high school and they were talking in the grocery store, and his friend says, "Oh my gosh, your wife . . . you're Valerie's husband." My husband replied, "Yes, I am. How do you know Valerie?" The friend explained that he knew I work with Knighton Real Estate advisors. "I see her stuff everywhere, so I just realized now you're Valerie's husband." My husband said, "That's right." (My husband, my biggest fan, would typically say, "Yeah, if you know anyone who's looking to buy, sell, or invest in Real Estate, she's your gal."). He always pumps our tires, which I love. In this particular case, not so much.

He thanks the guy, returned home and said, "Wow, so my friend from high school knows you." He shared his name, and I'm like, "I don't know who he is." My husband explains that the guy knew me from social media and the Real Estate team, and kept calling him Valerie's husband, and not Jason. We laughed, and I share that story now because it's just a perfect example of how our branding has reached the mass markets and has generated exposure for our team.

The second story I want to share with you is on mailouts. When I first started on the team, we were doing mailouts. At the time, we were only sending 1,200 mailouts to a small little farm area in my team leader's community. Again, it was just the two of us at this time. Once a month, I would create the marketing mailout, send it off to the printers, and then go pick them up. Then I'd bring them back and coil them in stacks of one hundred, or more. It would take hours. I would have elastic bands snapping in my hands, and I was cursing in my head. It was a job that I didn't envy doing, but it had to be done and there was no one else to do it. It was my job to do. I would then pack them up with the boxes and take them to Canada Post with delegated postal codes to send out to our farm area. As we grew, we had to expand that. We started doing 5,000 mailouts; one hundred per stack, elastic band, put in a box, and taken to the post office. We started with maybe three boxes and got up to six boxes.

Just know that I did it every single day with a smile on my face because it was my job, and I knew the benefits of doing this. We were looking to create brand exposure and build brand recognition for ourselves in our farm area. I was just about three, maybe four, months into my role and I said to my team leader, "If we are serious about our ROI, I would love to remove one piece of marketing from our list, and it would be our mailouts. No one calls about them. I know a lot of people complain about them because it's just another recycling piece they have to throw in the box. I think that we maybe shouldn't do them anymore." I was getting ready to jump for joy, thinking he would agree. Then, we get a phone call the next day from a lady who keeps getting our mailouts; she is now ready to list her property. So, hand to my heart, I solemnly swore that I will continue doing the mailouts because it reached one person, one listing pays for the marketing we do monthly. The whole purpose is exposure and building our brand awareness. This is the reason we don't easily give up on it.

Gage your ROI on each thing you do. There has to be a Return on Investment. I believe everything has to have an ROI on it. So, it was at the point where we were four months in and there was no ROI coming. More blood, sweat, tears and paper cuts from those thick pieces of paper, not just regular paper. Yes, I'm complaining because I want you to understand how much I did not enjoy that part of my job. I was waiting for the moment to talk about the ROI on this, then that call came in. Then another call came in.

Each year we now average seven to eight leads strictly from our mailouts. Now it has become a lesson learned story we share with all new agents looking to build a farm area. We even joke about how I wanted to give up so easily.

I'm going to share another story on how much branding we get from this method. I'm a hockey mom, and most of my hockey mom friends are in this farm area that we send our mailouts to. My hockey moms (shout out to my Hockey Moms) bring the mailout, that we send out monthly, to our hockey practices and ask me to autograph it. Sometimes we'll put a team photo on it and they think it's hilarious, but they don't throw it out. They keep it because they see my photo and they want to support me. I am so glad we didn't give up on those mailouts.

I now know, based on experience, it typically takes anywhere from three to six months to gain exposure in many things we do, and because this one particular thing—our mailouts—is only being sent out once a month, it needed a little bit more time to build its own brand awareness. To this day, we have upped our mailout game to 10,000 pieces. I do not do these by hand anymore. We have a marketing firm that does the printing, binding and mailing of our mailouts. All I have to do is see if it is in my mailbox. It's glorious and I love it. I'm so glad that I continued to do it.

What do you do for your Agents? Do you go the distance? There will be jobs that you don't like. The Agents will do things that you don't like. It's all part of the grind. It's all part of our career. We have this amazing role where we can reach thousands of people each week. We have the opportunity to work with so many amazing people and help so many families.

When the days are long, and you are in the middle of the worst job you could ever possibly imagine doing, I want you to remember my marketing story. Let's share some of those crazy moments where it's the part of the job that you don't enjoy all the time. I want you to take a photo of you doing that job, tag me in it on social media, and share because chances are, I'm probably doing one of those jobs that day as well, and

I will share my experience back. It's the reward at the end, the payout, that one phone call that came at the right time led me to know how important systems and ROIs are.

CHAPTER 9

TRACKING NUMBERS

Success Indicators

lright, we've made it to chapter nine; one of the best topics in the entire book. Some Agents obsess over what we are about to talk about. I've never met a realtor who didn't love knowing their stats and who didn't track their numbers. If you're reading this and don't track your numbers, there's nothing wrong with that. You're going to start now because you've added an Admin to your team, or some of you are thinking of growing a team or adding to it. It's important to know last year's numbers and this year's numbers. It all goes hand in hand with budget, goal planning, etc.

If you remember in chapter three, we put together your goals. Some of you will track GCI goals. Some of you will track unit goals, and that's okay. Track whatever it is you plan on tracking. We're going to talk about GCI, which is Gross Commission Income. What does that number look like, and how do you get there? Your brain might explode during this chapter because it's really important to understand the breakdown of how you get to your goals.

I want to take a minute and go back to chapter three. I want you to pull out the goals you planned during that chapter. Some of you might not have even taken the opportunity to do that—I'm hoping you did. If you followed the basic formula of Average Commission, I gave a very even number of $10,000, multiplied by your units you projected for yourself, that equals your GCI. To get to your GCI goal, play around with your units projected. If your goal of $10,000 Average Commissions is multiplied by twenty-five product units, this equals your GCI; you're going to want to take it one step further. Once you've established your GCI goal, and just say it's $100,000, write it down. I want you to get a whiteboard because what you're going to do is share that number with your Admin. Now it's their goal too, and they're going to help you reach it.

You've established that you need to sell a set number of units to reach your goal of $100,000. Get a big whiteboard, and honestly, I know you realtors love whiteboards, so you probably have eight already. If that's the case, delegate one whiteboard to lead-tracking. I might make your head spin a little bit here, so just bear with me. Get a tracking sheet or board, and then create columns. You can do it monthly or weekly, whatever it is that makes you feel comfortable. You're going to track your appointments booked and appointments went on. How many contacts you've added to the database and how many lead-gen hours you put in.

You're probably asking why is all that important. It is because you find your gaps. When you're trying to reach a GCI goal, you want to keep track of all of the other things you're doing. If you remember my database chapter on how many contacts you add to your database, and how many appointments you book, it keeps you on the right track.

Next, you need to ask yourself, "How many appointments do I need to go on to get to my units' goal. How many calls do I need to make to get those appointments booked?"

I want you to remember that you may have to start backward and move your way to the start, to get to your end results. This graph will show you how to it's going to break down and tell you how many appointments you need to go on to reach your GCI goal.

If you've hung on this long and you've committed to tracking your numbers, we're on the right track. In the next part of this chapter, we're going to talk about breaking down goals, setting goals, how to document them, the importance of a whiteboard, and why it's important to track your numbers.

Revisit last year's numbers so you can look back on it and say, "I was able to do twenty units last year. This year I've got an Admin, so I'm not tied down on all the back-office stuff. I can actually focus on building the business and commit more to lead-gen hours, more follow-ups, more negotiating contracts, more going on appointments, and more networking events." It's safe to say that you could probably double your business when you have an Administrator. Going into this year and completing this book, you should be thinking about next year's business planning. Keep track of your numbers so you can plan for when you sit down and do business planning for the next year.

Why is it important to have a goal and track it? It's our business indicator. How many of us have tried to do something without reading the manual first, like putting together an IKEA desk with no instructions. You will eventually get it built, but it may not be sturdy or last long, and there are probably some leftover screws and a wobbly leg. Well, if you continue to build a business without goals, how do you know where you are or where you want to be? How do you know you have achieved your milestones? How do you know it's time to expand and grow? You will have an idea, but you really won't have an end game. Also, it's messy without goals and visions. It's also not a sustainable business.

Lead-Generation

As we jump into the next part of this chapter, which is all about number tracking, we want to take the goals that we have and break them down. We want to start talking about the GCI goal. How many appointments do we need to book? How many calls do we need to make? You create your system from there, breaking down the goals so that they're understandable, attainable, and you can share that information with others in a way that everyone can relate to. This is extremely important. Take your units from last year. You're going to track last year's numbers over this year's numbers.

Let's say you closed twenty deals last year. This year you have an Admin. You're not going to be tied down in all the backend stuff. You have your amazing Administrator to do all that stuff for you, which means more opportunity to lead-gen, networking, going on appointments, contacting new clients, negotiating contracts—all of the big jobs. The reality of it is, with an Admin, you should be able to double your business.

If you know that last year you did twenty deals, what's going to be your magic number to increase your business this year? Are you going to add only five more deals to that or are you going to go big, think big, and say, "I can double my business; I'm going to go for forty units this year. I'm going to help forty families!" You don't know until you track. If you don't know how to find last year's numbers because you didn't have anyone helping you, contact the brokerage you are with and ask for last year's stats. They will have that information. They might also be able to track your sales volume average and the number of days on the market, all that fun stuff.

Average days on the market is a great tool to use during a listing appointment to be able to sit with the client and say, "You know, the average days on the market in our market centre is twenty to twenty-five days, but I average around twelve to thirteen days." Those are amazing stats. Again, it comes back to the importance of tracking. You're getting closer with your stats from last year, which is your goal for this year. Next up, reviewing how many new contacts you've added into the database.

This is going to be a key piece on how you will be able to project your business. What you should do when planning for next year, instead of just saying, "I'm going to add twenty units," indicate how you plan to get those twenty units. You look back and say, how many new contacts did I add into the database this year? This year shows your growth. It's also an indicator of how you are increasing your business. What new lead-gen do you need to add to your business to feed your database to get you to your unit goal, and your GCI goal? It's important to know how many people you have added to the database.

When we talk about the database, you take your average client in your database and multiply by how many deals they've done with you, so far. Some of you are sitting on a goldmine. You never want to look at a client like they are dollars and cents or a commission cheque, like I mentioned before. However, the reality of it is once you start recognizing those lead indicators, it's a great motivator to push you forward.

As an Admin, I'm always tracking our referral sources in our database. Where's the most value? If a client I know refers business to us, like crazy, I will answer every time they call. They are the first person that gets access to our VIP events, as well. Keep treating them well. Knowing how many people are in your database is very important and is a key measure to your growth and the health of your database.

As we move through this chapter, I'm going to give you tips and tools that you can use. This is the bare basics to start a foundation of lead-tracking. If you're committed to lead-tracking, I'm going to ask you to commit your Admin to it, too. Discuss the numbers with your Admin.

We're going to break down your goals, how to get to your goal systems for tracking, how often to review numbers and celebrate the wins. Let's start at number tracking and what to track.

Did you pick a unit goal or GCI goal? We will use GCI and even numbers for this example. Also, these numbers will be after splits. I don't want to confuse anyone over simple number tracking. An Average Commission of $10,000, multiplied by the number of units projected, equals your GCI, after splits. Let's say your goal is $100,000. Based on an Average Commission of $10,000, how many units do you need to sell to get to your GCI goal?

Once you have established that, write it down. Get a whiteboard and dedicate it to just number tracking. Next, you need to ask, "How many appointments do I need to go on to get to my goal of units?" Then, it's, "How many calls do I need to make to get those appointments booked?" Ideally, you want to be purposeful with your day and year, and it all comes down to your numbers. Establish goals. Lead-gen goals will accelerate your thought process and energize you to get the business. You need to remember not to get too aggressive with your goals, especially if you haven't tracked before.

Quick Tip: Take your units from last year—let's say it was twenty. You want to increase business this year, so take that twenty and then think about how much you can increase your business. Would it be 1.5 percent? The number of new contacts in your database will show your growth and indicate how you are increasing your business. What new methods of lead-gen did you add to your business? Use those tools to analyze what a good number is to increase your business.

The next step in tracking is how to track and where. A good starting point is an Excel spreadsheet. Start small and build it out as you grow. Another method is writing them down, daily. How many contacts added, appointments booked, and deals closed? Then there is also the whiteboard—the visual component. It will always be a reminder, right in front of you, and your team will see the progress, as well. It's important to have one of these systems in place right now. This is where an Admin is needed. Admins, having a home for number tracking and knowing the numbers will set you apart from an average Admin. I'm reminding all Admins here; this is where your value shows. Understanding the numbers, how much is needed to keep the lights on, how many families you want to help, how much of an increase you want to see from last year. This chapter is giving you the basic model to grow you into a high-level Empire Builder.

One thing that has been super beneficial, in my career, is a success planner. We collaborated over the years with what we want to track and how we want to handle our tracked numbers. Then we were able to build a success planner that is branded to our team. I created one for Admins to help with income and expenses, help track numbers and keep you focused on the daily tasks at hand. Every month you look at the month before, find the gaps in your business, and set yourself up for the new month. Whatever goals you didn't hit from the previous month won't disappear. They carry over. Don't get heavy shoulders because you didn't track your numbers. Every Monday, review the numbers for the week and what it will take to get you there. YOU, the Admin, have to get in front of your sphere to help grow your numbers. Don't forget that you can sell your team, as well.

After Lead-Gen

I want to take a minute and share a brief story with you about our team. It's going to sound like over communication and constant number checking, and, to be honest, it is. Ok, hold up . . . I just want to back track here and explain how we track our numbers. Every Sunday, our Agents sit down, plan out their week, look at the numbers they need for this week and look at where they currently sit, knowing that going into Monday we're going to share those numbers as a team. We have a wig session, which stands for Wildly Important Goals, and every Monday we talk about those goals. We check in on one another to discuss where our weaknesses were and why we didn't reach our goal. Then for others, why we were successful in hitting our goals? Was it a successful Open House, etc.?

Our team takes it one step further by tracking monthly, as well. We call it the 15th protocol. Not only do we check in on each other every single Monday and do our planning on Sundays, but we also check in on the 15th of every month to discuss where we are for the mid-month. It gives us an idea if we're ahead or behind, where we need to increase lead-gen, what we could do to get to our goal or if we're surpassing our goal. Do we add to the goal for that month or are we consistent enough with our activities?

It might sound crazy for us to sit and review our numbers, as much as we do, but the evidence to success is really in the numbers and having that 15th protocol of every month and doing our mid-month review opens our eyes and holds us accountable. It motivates other team members who are not close to them, or just a deal shy of hitting their goal for the month. For those who aren't very great at tracking numbers and holding ourselves accountable to our goals, it's a great accountability piece for a team. So, for those Agents who struggle with tracking the numbers and taking the time to do that, we're holding them accountable. And, by checking in, we can identify if they're one deal away from hitting their goal or if they've surpassed it. It gives us a heads up on what the next two weeks of that month should look like and, more importantly, what we can do to support the Agent. As a business owner, numbers are always your priority and including your Admin in on this empowers them to understand the business' importance.

How does your Admin leverage this for you? How do you utilize your Admin in the world of tracking numbers? It's simple. I track my numbers, as well. I have my own goals. I know my Agent's goals because I hang them above my desk, where I sit, so I'm constantly looking at them. I break them down quarterly, and then from quarterly, I break them down monthly. I know, at the beginning of every month, what our goal is for that month.

Why do I do that? I do it because I care, a lot. I care about the success of our Agents. It has nothing to do with money. Like I've said, I'm not motivated by money. I just enjoy watching them succeed. High-level Administrators hold their Agents to extreme accountability around numbers, as well as tracking them. Same goes for lead-gen. If an Agent comes to a meeting that we're going to have about our numbers and goals, and doesn't have that information in front of them, we ask them to leave the meeting or get their numbers. We need to keep that mindset fresh and understand the importance behind number tracking and goal planning. If you've made it through this chapter and I haven't lost you, or I have got you excited about tracking numbers, then you're going to love the next part. So, get ready!

Celebrate the Numbers

Celebrate the numbers; small wins are still wins. Big wins are even better. Celebrate the milestones. I know you realtors love to have fun. You love any opportunity to celebrate life and just interact with others in a fun atmosphere. You're going to like this part of the chapter because I'm going to give you reasons to have some fun. As you plan your yearly goals and break them down monthly, and quarterly, I want you to also think of how you celebrate the milestones. I don't mean just when you reach your goals. Celebrate the milestones. If you have new Agents on your team, celebrate their first deal. Celebrate client reviews, hitting your monthly goal, hitting your weekly targets, booking an appointment during the day, and so on.

This part of the chapter will give you some ideas on how to celebrate and how to know if it's a celebration or a put your head down and keep going kind of day. If you're having a terrible year and your thoughts are that there's nothing to celebrate, but yet, the reality is you are hanging on with your head down and you're grinding it out daily. Doing the actions that you need to do, that's a reason to celebrate in my eyes.

Showing up is part of it and then you keep pushing yourself. Celebrate the small victories. It's showing up every day to get you to your goals.

I always tell the Admins that I coach to plan an event every quarter. Normally, I like to close out the chapter with a story, but I'm going to tell you a story now. Every quarter I plan what we call "team advances," for our team. I make it a big deal and a surprise. I would say, "If you guys do well this quarter, we're going to do an event, and we go all out." I've rented out one of the most haunted places in our area. It was completely shut down just for our team for a private dinner with a crew from the space channel. They came in and showed us what a ghost tour looks like because our team just needed to unwind and have some fun, not work-related, nor Real Estate related.

As our team grew, we needed to be more purposeful with our goal planning, so now at our team's Year End review we break down our team events, and we tell them ahead of time. We mention we will hold two major team advances and four smaller team retreats; we have these events planned out and share the idea with the team. We still keep it as a surprise. These events are for everyone, not just the ones who have a successful month or year. We celebrate everything as a team.

These events are meant for relaxing and celebrating each other. I can give you a list of some amazing team advances and great ways to have fun. If it's just you and your Admin right now, it's as simple as having a tea, having a lunch break together or going to a nice restaurant and celebrating a great month. Make it a monthly routine. It could even be a spa day you want to give your Admin. If you haven't done that for your

Admin, write it down and do it as soon as you can. It's probably one of my favourite things to do.

Our team has an Administrative team of four wonderful ladies who bring their A-game every day. In their contracts, I have it separate that I will plan two Admin retreats a year. One will be Real Estate related, where we go to a conference and we learn. The second one is a wellness retreat, and we get that when we reach our goals. Now, mind you, our goals are slightly different than an Agent's goals, but still worth celebrating. They work harder than any other Administrative team and deserve every bit of celebration.

To Summarize: How to Celebrate the Numbers

Admins, I want you to grab a pen and a piece of paper, because ideas will flow. You're going to love it. One of the things that were hard for our team was COVID-19. The global pandemic forced our team, which is very close, to be separated all over the city and the only connection we had to one another was Zoom. We closed our office in March, 2020, and we had our June team advances planned. It was in the contract. Our team did well. We pivoted and shifted so hard during the pandemic that we did not have to lay anyone off. We we're very fortunate.

One thing we strongly believed in was that COVID-19 wasn't going to take our spark, our energy that we all bring to the team, so we were determined we would celebrate our pivot in the virtual world. One of the things that we thought about was HOW? How do we celebrate our team right now? Are we going to be able to give this team a team advance? We are just sitting here on Zoom calls. We realized we needed to change our way of thinking.

We have a pretty big goal. One thing we did when COVID-19 hit was that we did not stop. Our goal did not shrink. We decided that we deserved to celebrate these small victories throughout this pandemic, still hitting our sales targets and helping others. We pivoted fast into a virtual-only world. So, how do we keep a team motivated, celebrating the victory and pushing through COVID-19? I love planning events because I love nothing more than seeing the smile on our team's faces. It's like a mom and her babies, and I know that sounds so cheesy, but I truly love spoiling them every chance I can get.

This was hard for me because I was worried that we couldn't be together for a team event, which our team enjoys. I wrote down every team member's name, and beside their name I wrote somebody's name down who is very influential in our world, whom of which they look up to. Think Ryan Serhant, he's wonderful but, unrealistically, I knew that he would never do a Zoom call with our team. I am not going to lie, I tried! What I did was, I wrote down a list of people that inspire our team. People we often quote, Authors we admire, and I sent a message to every single one of those people. I said, "Listen, we're in this pandemic together and before we get Zoomed out, what would it take to get you on a call with my team who could use little bit of inspiration to keep pushing because we have a really big goal? What can we do? What can I do to get you in front of my team?" I'll be honest, out of the ten people, I connected with nine. I had responses like, "Yes! I would love to connect with other people, and I'm thankful that I'm somebody who inspires your team because I need a little bit of inspiration."

I had people in Europe. I had social media influencers in Real Estate. We did our Zoom calls during COVID-19; we held our meetings on Mondays, Wednesdays and Fridays. Every Wednesday, I surprised them with a guest speaker. They had no idea they would get on the Zoom call and that person would be there. We took so many notes and it kept us going. We took something, such as the pandemic, and we switched the way we look at it.

I don't want to take away from any of the bad things that have happened to people. We've all been hit by COVID-19 in some way, shape, or form, but I also don't want to take away from the good stuff that COVID-19 gave us either. It allowed us to have real conversations with people that inspire us. As soon as we approached the end of summer, which was August of 2020, we were in phase three and we could open things up, so I decided to throw an event to get us all familiar with each other again, since we had been living in a virtual environment for months.

Phones sat at the desk during the event, so nobody was on their phone. We started with yoga meditation and then moved into this amazing catered dinner. We had wellness boxes in place for all the Agents with a little treat from us just to thank them for showing up every day. The whole point of this part of the chapter, on celebrating the numbers, is to share with you that celebrating milestones and celebrating small steps is important as you grow a team, no matter the size.

My Agent and I—when it was just the two of us—would go to lunch together, or he would take me to dinner, or he would buy me my favourite bottle of wine just to say thank you and to celebrate. We exchanged inspirational little notes and we read books together. We'd get each other books as gifts and it was just to say, "Hey, you're doing a great job and it's not going unnoticed." We must do that!

I hope you grabbed that pen and paper, and I hope you have a sheet full of ideas. For this chapter, your homework is planning one amazing team event, or advance, celebrating the entire year if it's close to the Year-End. Celebrate mid-year review, if it's the middle of the year, or if you just came off an incredibly successful month. Find a reason to celebrate. I'm going to give you a few other examples on a smaller scale, so hang on to that pen and piece of paper and take notes.

As you plan your yearly goals, and break them down monthly and quarterly, I want you to also think of how you will celebrate the milestones. I don't mean just when you reach your goals. Don't worry if you think your Agent won't participate in this or thinks it's silly. We will work on that. Every quarter when your team reaches its goal or surpasses it, celebrate with a team get together, even if it's just the two of you. Plan a lunch together or cheers with a glass of wine at the end of the day. Add a small gift to you both as a job well done.

As a team, celebrate with a team dinner. Reward your team with a small token of appreciation, such as some new branded swag, personalized water bottles, etc. Celebrate your first deal, monthly wins, the first week you book all your appointments or hit your goals, the first time you get a lead from Facebook. Track milestones and celebrate them.

A team member finally got a call from a family member to help with selling their home. This is the first time a family member has given them the opportunity because they were worried about the family relationship. They knocked it out of the park and opened the door for others to be comfortable. *Huge win* for the team and that needed to be celebrated.

Last tip of the chapter, hold an annual event. A business planning meeting that focuses on, and highlights, what is to come for the next year. I encourage everyone, in October, to sit down and start goal planning for the next year. Make it a big deal, hold a meeting (even if it's just the two of you), plan and share.

One thing I don't stress a lot about in this book is the growth of a large team, and a lot of the systems and models I talk about are ground up because you need to build these models out first. Before adding more talent to your team, you need an attractive and appealing foundation for other Agents.

CHAPTER 10

LESSONS LEARNED

As I close out this book, I want us to wind down together. I want to share my journey on how I got here, and why I think it's important for all Admins to be treated as equals. Five years ago, I was given the opportunity to work with a gentleman by the name of Chris Knighton. I mentioned him earlier. He has big goals, big visions, and works harder than any other Real Estate Agent I know to build a substantial business for everyone around us.

Going through the last five years with this team, I should be saying how hard it was and share a lot of struggles, but the truth is, outside of reaching goals and helping over 800 families, this journey has been amazing. WHY? Because I found my passion, and when you find that it isn't a job for you anymore. I never felt it was, and Chris certainly never treated me like it was.

It starts at the beginning. How you treat that first hire will be the voice of how you treat your clients, if you ask me. Lead with a servant's heart and know that it comes down to working with people who share the vision and can help you get there.

I was given a major opportunity to build the foundation of Canada's top team within our brokerage. We sit at #1 in our local market centre and at 1 percent in our Real Estate board. We got there using the systems I have shared in this book. We need systems, hard work, and passion for what we do.

We created an MVV that we stand behind in all areas of our business, and I never once felt like "just an Admin." That isn't our culture. My obstacles, that aren't even mine, are listening to other Admins struggles. They need this to work, but their Agent isn't the greatest mentor or leader. They are treated like paper-pushers for the Agent and are asked to be seen and not heard. I can't even imagine living and working like this, and I am so sorry to anyone who feels this way. If you are reading this and feeling this way about your Agent, I want you to email me and I will help you communicate with your Agent. I also want you to be honest with yourself and hold yourself accountable to what the bigger issue might be and be prepared that a conversation is needed for you and your Agent.

I knew two years ago that the next steps in life were mentoring, leading, teaching, training and coaching other Admins within our community. We all deserve to feel how I feel every day at work, how it can be a career for you and not just a job. I am making it my mission to help both Agents and Admins see the value in a partnership. Learning about the visionary and integrator role, and, more importantly, I love watching Admins grow into Empire Builders.

Along my travels, I have been trained by some of the most amazing minds within Real Estate. Keller Williams opened my eyes, built my confidence, and supported me every step of the way. I want to make sure that I share it with the world. I really would not be where I am today if one lady out there hadn't answered my email about the job they were hiring for.

I was in a spot in life where I wasn't happy with my career. I was in the banking industry and they were laying off amazing employees, neglecting clients' real needs, and changing what was truly important to us and the way we do business. I wouldn't say I disliked it, and I always said I would never work where I am not happy. I'm not motivated by money. It's great, but happiness motivates me. Seeing others happy takes it to the next level. So, I left the bank and all its comforts to start brand new.

From day one, I knew I would never look back. From my first meeting with the most wonderful lady to my first meeting with Chris, I knew this is where I needed to be. I won't bore you with all the small details; you can get one-on-one with me after this if you want to learn more about our brokerage.

How did I get here? Let's backtrack for a minute. What makes me credible and gives me the confidence to write this book? In the last four years, I have taken four courses around the perfect Real Estate Assistant and encouraged my team leader to continue to attend. I have joined one of the most amazing coaching companies for Real Estate Agents. I have been on stage talking about systems and held classes with over sixty admins in attendance. I have met some of the most influential people in Real Estate who have coached me, personally, and pushed me to keep going. I have learned more than systems and models in Real Estate. I learned how to read people, script practice, role-play for objective handling, and how to build a life worth living. I will share all of my top skills with you.

I will continue to keep going because I want every Agent to know that we, the Administrators, are your secret weapon in Real Estate and I will empower your Admin to push you to the next level, and then the next, and just when you think you can't get any further, we will break the ceiling so you can keep going. We got you! Trust us. Let us show you what we can do. To my future and present Empire Builders, remove "just an admin" from your vocabulary and when anyone asks you what you do, I want you to say, "Oh, I'm an Empire Builder for (such and such) Real Estate Agent in (your city)." People will ask you, "What is an Empire Builder?" And now you know how to answer that, proudly.

This journey isn't done for us because there is so much more to share. This is the beginning of what will be a beautiful friendship of trust, confidence-building, and, more importantly, Empire Building. Hold on to your notepad, vision and goals because, with hard work and passion, we will move mountains in Real Estate.

At the end of every chapter, I have left you with some homework. By taking these small steps towards building a foundation, you will have an incredible start to your business. However, you are only as strong as your weakest link…don't let it be YOU!

Take the homework and implement it one at a time. One of the things that we do as Admins is, we try to do it all at once and that is a huge set up for failure. You cannot do it all at once. You can, however, do it all. I will personally work with you to implement all you need and want to do, but for now just write down five things you would like to implement. Right now, write them down. Once you are done, pick one that you want to start right away. Take that item and build it out—how to implement it and when to implement it—test it or go with it. Whatever you do, document it.

As you go, you will write that famous Operations Manual every company should have. I am giving you one of the biggest tips *ever* right here. Everything you do from this moment on *document it*, and you will have completed your Operations Manual (if I could take a time machine back five years to tell myself this little gold nugget, I would one hundred times over).

When you've completed reading this book, I want you both, Agents and Admins, to schedule a thirty-minute brain dump, work together and share AHA moments from this book . . . *then* I want to hear your AHAs.

I've dedicated the last paragraph to all of the Admins out there who strive to be the best version of yourselves, every day. Who show up every day because this is a career for you and one that you love. I have one statement for you . . .You Rock! On those days when you feel unappreciated, your communication has broken down with your Agent, and you almost wonder if it's worth it, I want you to pull out this book and read this last paragraph as many times as you need to.

This is not an easy role and don't let anyone tell you differently. You will wear multiple hats, and you will be misunderstood because it's hard for some people to believe that we would care about someone else's business, but the truth is it's not just theirs. You have made it your own, and I am super proud of who you are.

If you implement any of the methods in this book and you have a success story to share, reach out to me and share it. We are going to create our own movement. It's time people saw and heard just how incredible we are and how we have been the secret weapon to a successful Real Estate business this whole time.

Go crush it! Go be positive! Go Build your Empire, and always remember that YOU'VE GOT THIS!

V

ACKNOWLEDGMENTS

Thank you, Jason. You are the reason this book is in people's hands. You not only supported me, but you also gave me the push of confidence to put my thoughts into print.

To my three amazing little men: Colm, Cael, and Colton. This book is to show you that you can do anything you put your mind to. Don't let anyone control your thoughts or actions. Go out into the world and empower and inspire those around you by your actions. I love you all very, very much.

I think back to the day Jason was swimming in our pool with our boys and I told him about the book opportunity. He didn't even hesitate, he said, "You need to do this, so go email them and tell them you are in." And here we are today.

To my team, I wouldn't have words to write this book if it weren't for every single one of you.

Thank you to Chris Knighton for empowering me day one. That is what separates us from the average. You knew who you needed in your business and you let me be that person and we have built a pretty powerful business. You created a culture that others can only try to replicate and you created an Empire Builder in me. Thank you for all you do and all your support.

To our Operations team: Shannon, Montana, Megan, and all of you that have made an impact in my life, thank you for allowing me to explore new ideas and to grow with me while we implement.

To my Empire Builders reading this book, thank you for supporting me, thank you for showing up every day and I hope this book is exactly what you needed to keep pushing forward.

This book is for each and every one of you.

I would love to express my thanks to my editor, Sarah Kramer, and my publisher, Morgan James Publishing, for all your guidance, support, and seeing the worth in this book.

THANK YOU

If you have made it this far and you still want more, here is how you can connect with me:
www.elitebosscoaching.com

For Coaching/Mastermind Inquiries:
valerie@elitebosscoaching.com

Join our Facebook Community:
https://www.facebook.com/groups/empirebuildersinrealestate

This is just the start of what I believe will be the most powerful community I have ever been a part of. I plan on building Empire Builders out of everyone I have the opportunity to work with.

ABOUT THE AUTHOR

Valerie Simoneau is proudly Canadian, living in the heart of Ontario just minutes away from the Wineries of the Niagara region. For the past five years she has mentored, trained, and coached some of the most elite Real Estate Administrators, in all of Canada, and works with some incredible powerhouse women building a career of their own. It is a huge passion of Valerie's to empower other women to create a career out of what they thought was a job.

Valerie has been on multiple podcasts and has spoken at numerous events within the Real Estate Community. She also runs one of the top Real Estate Admin Masterminds in Canada, within Keller Williams Real Estate. Valerie has been featured in *Mompreneur* Magazine and has been nominated twice for Mompreneur of the Year in Canada. She is the Director of Operations for one of the top three teams in Keller Williams Canada. This is home to the foundation of the systems and models Valerie talks about in Empire Builders.

A free ebook edition is available with the purchase of this book.

To claim your free ebook edition:

1. Visit MorganJamesBOGO.com
2. Sign your name CLEARLY in the space
3. Complete the form and submit a photo of the entire copyright page
4. You or your friend can download the ebook to your preferred device

A **FREE** ebook edition is available for you or a friend with the purchase of this print book.

CLEARLY SIGN YOUR NAME ABOVE

Instructions to claim your free ebook edition:
1. Visit MorganJamesBOGO.com
2. Sign your name CLEARLY in the space above
3. Complete the form and submit a photo of this entire page
4. You or your friend can download the ebook to your preferred device

Print & Digital Together Forever.

Snap a photo

Free ebook

Read anywhere

CPSIA information can be obtained
at www.ICGtesting.com
Printed in the USA
JSHW042256131221
21261JS00002B/44